Forward by Bishop Emeritus, Donald W. Trautman

"It is not very often that a book can reach into your heart and move you."

— Jim Kelly

is Stronger than Pain

Based on the Inspirational True Story of

Irene Corcoran O'Brien

As Remembered by Her Son

MICHAEL J. O'BRIEN

LOVE IS STRONGER THAN PAIN
BASED ON THE INSPIRATIONAL TRUE STORY OF IRENE CORCORAN O'BRIEN AS REMEMBERED BY HER SON MICHAEL J. O'BRIEN

iUniverse books may be ordered through booksellers or by contacting:

iUniverse
1663 Liberty Drive
Bloomington, IN 47403
www.iuniverse.com
1-800-Authors (1-800-288-4677)

ISBN: 978-1-4917-8226-2 (sc)
ISBN: 978-1-4917-8225-5 (hc)
ISBN: 978-1-4917-8224-8 (e)

Library of Congress Control Number: 2015920674

Print information available on the last page.

iUniverse rev. date: 1/29/2016

Contents

Foreword

Dear Reader,

If you have ever felt abandoned by God, if you have ever questioned God's will for you, if you have ever experienced one cross, one tragedy, one affliction after another, if you have ever had your prayers go unanswered, then this book is a "must" for you.

Love is Stronger Than Pain is not a pious story but a true, authentic account of a wife and mother whose faith and perseverance were heroic. She raised eight children, two of whom were invalids born with a rare skin disease needing her constant care. She coped with the tragic accidental death of her twenty year old son, the death of her beloved husband, a fire in the family home, the death of her parents, all within the span of a few years. In all of this she suffered enormously, but never doubted the love of God and always had love for those in need. Her faith and endurance were tested beyond limits, and yet she persisted in faith and trust in God. Irene O'Brien is a modern day Job. We all need to learn from this faith filled woman that her suffering produced perseverance and that perseverance produced hope.

Well written and easy reading, this book will lead you in places to tears and a deeper faith and understanding of God's will. Clear and compelling, her son Michael has written from first hand knowledge. May we all grow in hope - the courage to be in the circumstances where we find ourselves. Please Lord, give us that courage.

Most Rev. Donald W. Trautman, STD, SSL
Bishop Emeritus

Acknowledgements

First and foremost, I am indebted to a dear friend and colleague, Michael K. Higgins. Michael assumed the arduous task of grappling with the first edit of this book.

I also want to acknowledge the assistance of Jacque Waggoner, CEO of Hunter's Hope. Jacque was of invaluable assistance in too many ways to enumerate. She also contributed to editing final copies of the manuscript.

I am deeply indebted to my sister-in-law, Jeanne O'Brien, for her laborious effort in finalizing the edits of the book. Jeanne was most pleasant throughout the entire process. It was a genuine labor of love.

A heartfelt thank you to my brother, Patrick. Patrick is recognized as the impeccable, family historian. Patrick not only assisted with dates, he also patiently uncovered family photographs that I was able to utilize in this book.

I would like to express my gratitude to my nephew, Richard. Richard's contributions were appreciated as he assisted his non-tech savvy Uncle Michael in transforming photographs to a digital format that he subsequently uploaded on my computer.

I want to thank three friends who encouraged me during the writing process. Tino, Sharon, and Mary Ann displayed genuine enthusiasm that provided the fuel I needed to continue with my endeavor.

Dedication

I dedicate this book to Laura Mae Fitzsimons Corcoran in whose presence I experienced profound peace. Additionally, she bestowed upon me a love for nature and the outdoors which lingers to this day as evidenced by my adventurous camping trips across this beautiful country. Most importantly, through her example, my grandmother instilled within me a deep, reverent, love for our Lord.

Additionally, I dedicate this book to my father Richard O'Brien. He exemplified service to the church. Every evening he sat at the kitchen table and served John and Maureen. He brought much joy to both of them as he performed what came to be known as their "nighttime ritual." There are not many men, if any at all, who could walk a mile in his shoes.

Finally, I dedicate this book to two dear friends Peg and Kate. They befriended Irene and John creating many, magical, moments that I will treasure all the days of my life.

All royalties from this book will be donated to:

- Hunter's Hope

Introduction

If you have ever felt so deeply compelled to accomplish something that you could not rest until the task was complete, then you will understand the depth of the drive I experienced to memorialize the life of my mother in *Love Is Stronger than Pain.* In short, using Catholic terminology, Irene O'Brien is worthy of being canonized a saint!

Irene endured trials and tribulations that would leave most wondering, "How could a loving God allow such suffering?" Indeed, the heartfelt pain of her tragedies may even have caused some to fall from their faith in the midst of such agony. However, Irene miraculously never imploded. Instead, she learned an important lesson about life and faith in the midst of her tribulations. Indeed, it was a painful and challenging lesson to learn. Yet, the lesson was one that edified her faith instead of destroying it. Irene's lesson in it's simplest terms was, "Learn for it to be sufficient for you to know the heart of God and not the mind of God." Irene loved her Lord and she remained convinced of His personal love for her. Irene's life was lived as a contemplation of the verse, "Love consists in this, not that we have loved God, but that He loved us" (1John 4:10).

Irene never wrote a book. She never even gave a public teaching. She was much too humble for that kind of attention. However, if you were ever fortunate enough to sit alone with her at the kitchen table, have her at the other end of your telephone line, or as a passenger in your car, you would undoubtedly consider yourself blessed to be the beneficiary of her unpretentious, invaluable wisdom.

As much as Irene's words consoled and encouraged multitudes of suffering hearts, it must be emphasized that it was her witness of life that had the most permanent impact on those who knew her personally or knew of her. Pope Paul VI, in his encyclical, *Evangelic Nuntiandi,* said it best, "Modern man listens more willingly to witnesses than to teachers, and if he does listen to teachers, it is because they are witnesses." Irene O'Brien did not merely "talk the talk," she "walked the walk" on a challenging, tumultuous journey that you can now follow in *Love Is Stronger than Pain.*

It is my hope and intention that through this book, Irene's legacy will continue to touch the hearts of those who suffer at the hands of the uninvited guest of personal tragedy. I am confident her words will impact every reader. I am even more confident that her witness of life contains the power to transform you. In her honor, all royalties from this book will be donated to charity.

Chapter One

IN THE BEGINNING, GOD CREATED INNOCENCE

It was one of the most brutally cold mornings of January 1934. The worn, walnut, RCA radio had its circular dial set on the only receivable station in the small rural town named Ovid, in the Finger Lakes region of New York State. The soothing, soft music, despite the occasional static, filled the kitchen with a warm ambiance that made one temporarily forget the raging storm outdoors. The magic of the music transmitted over the radio was interrupted by the CBS news, which was forecasting record low temperatures for this date in late January for all of Central New York State. Wind chill factors were being reported as well below zero. The blowing and drifting snow outside was causing near zero visibility. Snowbanks were already piled so high that some appeared as though they were mammoth glaciers, like those in Seward, Alaska.

Michael Corcoran had been up well before the light of dawn to assure the furnace was stoked with fresh coal to provide sufficient heat. The heat rose through a single floor register between the downstairs living room and dining room. A small vent in the ceiling directly above the register allowed some of the warm air to rise to the three upstairs bedrooms and the upstairs bathroom. Make no mistake, on a blustery morning like this, the upstairs remained as frigid as an igloo in the Arctic. Each of the wooden beds had several blankets topped with cozy, homemade quilts. Not a single, exposed body part of the children could be seen extending from any of the wool blankets. The Corcoran children looked like brown grizzlies nestled deep in hibernation. It was a wonder they did not suffocate under the heap of blankets piled on them. Pounds of blankets must have been placed on each bed.

Indeed, this particular morning was a virtual fight against the extreme elements of a cruel winter. Actually, the battle had been waged for an entire, grueling week caused by a large, arctic air mass descending from the North, gripping its sharp claws well into the South. Undoubtedly, this was causing everyone in the Corcoran family to grow tiresomely weary of a seemingly, endless, relentless winter. Irene, the second eldest of the five children, lay snuggled in her bed, half-awake, pleasantly dreaming of the arrival of the warmth of spring, followed by the long, hot days of summer. Irene loved everything about summer. She listened intently to the dreadful, howling wind outside her bedroom window. *Today is January 30th. Thank God this trying month is almost over. Summer's glory draws nigh!*

Meanwhile, downstairs in the kitchen, Laura Mae Fitzsimons Corcoran, Michael's wonderful, hardworking wife exclaimed, "Michael Joseph, I vow that this summer, not a single complaint about the heat and humidity shall pass my lips, so help me God. And should any complaints inadvertently slip out, please feel free to chastise me by reminding me of this very morning."

Laura had the white, General Electric, gas oven turned up to 450 degrees with the oven door wide open. Additionally, all the top burners were turned on high in a desperate attempt to provide additional heat in the kitchen, before the children were awakened and called down for breakfast. Lamps had been placed near the plumbing overnight to prevent pipes from breaking. Still, drafts could be felt through the bottom of the doors and even through the paper that was adhered to each of the kitchen windows to provide additional insulation.

"Never underestimate the power of mother nature," Laura muttered to herself. "She has a nasty temper and a will of her own that leaves us completely at her mercy without even so much as a warning. All we can do is find a way to cope with the unpredictable storms that she sends our way, so we can survive. That often requires deep faith."

Laura fixed Michael a hearty breakfast of her famous buttermilk pancakes, smothered with freshly churned butter, and covered with warm maple syrup. A side of thickly sliced bacon and toast filled Michael's plate. Laura also packed a lunch for her husband to take with him as he departed for work. Immediately upon his departure, Laura Mae busily began setting the five-legged, white, porcelain-topped kitchen table for her four children that were of school age. The four older children were Glenn, Irene, Leo, and Joyce. Mickey was the "caboose," the baby. Both leafs of the table were extended, as mismatched placemats and ceramic bowls of various colors were carefully placed on the only table in the household. The over-used table wobbled just a little on the kitchen's black and white tiled floor. A pitcher of fresh cream, a box of Sun-made Raisins, a sugar bowl filled with Domino's Brown Sugar, and a shaker of ground cinnamon were quickly added to the table as if Laura had three hands instead of two. As Laura began boiling a big pot of water for the Quaker Oats, she added a large pinch of salt to the water, then quickly left the kitchen momentarily to lay the children's school clothes on the floor adjacent to the only register in the house, to warm them up a bit.

On her way back to the kitchen, Laura stopped at the bottom of the stairs, holding firmly onto the carved wooden railing. With her left hand cupped to her mouth, Laura called up the stairs, "Glenn, Irene, please get up. And wake your brother and sister. Breakfast is almost ready and it will take a lot of extra time to walk to school this morning."

This was Laura's morning routine from the bottom of the creaky, wooden stairs whose frequent wear revealed several coats of different colored paint. Laura Mae was a big woman and a strong one at that. Her "yell" up the stairs had a firm, yet whispered, raspy tone to it. The children loved being awakened by her frail yet firm voice. The children reluctantly, but obediently, scurried down the stairs and made a quick dash for the register where they knew they would find their warmed school clothes. Wearing their slippers and pajamas, and shivering so much that they looked like a lake trout out of the water, they stood on the register to warm up a bit before they even thought of dressing. Each child seemed to have their individually claimed territory in one of the four corners of the register. Then, in an instant, they were out of their pajamas and into their school clothes with such haste it was like a Houdini magic act.

The children loved the warm oatmeal breakfast served with Sunday's leftover, homemade cinnamon rolls. However, each of the children dreaded the idea of walking the two miles down Gilbert Road to the village school in such perilous conditions. There were no school buses in those days, at least not in this small, rural town. Additionally, school was seldom closed in those days. Irene resigned herself to the storm. *I guess it's all a part of God's plan for life and complaining doesn't make the situation any better.* As Glenn, Irene, Leo, and Joyce were finishing breakfast, they began to layer themselves in the warmest clothes they owned. Laura was just finishing the last school lunch. Reluctantly, each grabbed their lunch off the table, and in a tight huddle, pushed each other toward the kitchen door. No one was savoring the inevitable battle against the wicked elements on their long walk to school.

Laura was as insistent upon her children attending school daily as she was insistent upon them attending church on Sundays. Laura's intention was to instill in her children the value of a good, formal education as well as a devout faith. A formal education was something that circumstances beyond Laura's control had denied her. Because Laura's mother, Delia Timothy, as well as her father, Richard Fitzsimons, had immigrated from Ireland to seek labor and escape the long-lingering aftermath of the devastating Potato Famine, Laura's assistance was required in farming the land and caring for the animals on her brother Leo's farm. Therefore, she was adamant that her children would be blessed with that which eluded her. Laura was non-compromising that her children make the long journey to the school on Main Street by foot. No excuses were accepted unless it was substantiated by a fever. It was mandatory that the fever be registered on the thermometer. The thermometer could always readily be found, when necessary, in the rusty, first-aid kit securely stored in the bottom drawer of the bathroom vanity. Laura further insisted the children all arrive at school punctually as a matter of daily routine. Make no mistake, instilling a devout, personal faith in each of their children was a responsibility that Laura and Michael embraced with the utmost sincerity.

Although Laura was deprived of a formal education, she was nonetheless an extremely intelligent woman whose curriculum included her deep and reverent reflections on the lessons of life, in the context of her devout faith, based upon a personal relationship with the Lord. Laura acquired throughout her life, a priceless and precious wisdom possessed by only a few rare individuals. As a woman of quiet, respectful demeanor, Laura never "cast her pearls before swine." Rather, she had an innate, infallible ability to discern with whom, and exactly when, she would share her insights and wisdom. Naturally, all of Laura's children, and subsequently all of her grandchildren, were beneficiaries of Laura's wise insights if they cared to listen and heed her words.

To this day, a grandson possesses a letter found inside a card celebrating his thirteenth birthday. In that letter, Laura inscribed something the grandson shall never forget and shall always cherish. "Remember darling, there is an old saying, 'Write your virtues in stone using a chisel and write your vices in sand using a finger.' This way, the waters of Baptism and the mighty wind of the Holy Spirit will wash your vices clean from the sand, and the good Lord will recognize you only by your virtues indelibly engraved in stone. Additionally, in this manner, you will always be able to identify with certitude, your true friends. For the true friend, like the Lord, will also choose to know you by your virtues, being quick to forgive and forget your vices. Remain as far as east is from west, from those who for any reason, feel compelled to remind you of your vices. These are the ones of which the Lord speaks, 'How can you say to your brother, 'brother, let me take out the speck that is in your eye,' when you yourself do not see the log that is in your own eye' (Luke 6:42). Such people miss the solemnity of the words, 'Be merciful, just as your Father is merciful. And do not judge and you will not be judged; and do not condemn, and you will not be condemned; pardon, and you will be pardoned' (Luke 36,37). I love you with my whole heart, darling!"

As Alfred Lord Tennyson once said, "Knowledge comes, but wisdom lingers." Laura Mae Fitzsimmons Corcoran was a woman of incredible wisdom. It was this wisdom that compelled her to raise her children as devout Christians and to stress to each of them the importance of a formal education.

As Glenn opened the kitchen door for the dreaded, two-mile departure to school on this frigid, blustery morning, Laura quickly slammed the door shut and barricaded it with her large, outstretched arms. She firmly admonished her four children, "Don't you dare leave this house without saying your prayers!"

Laura was a devout Christian, not just on Sundays, but on weekdays also. The family cherished their faith and attempted to live it on a daily basis, incorporating morning and evening prayers as part of the family's daily regimen. Not a morsel of food better touch their lips before it was duly blessed. Both Laura and Michael were uncompromising and diligent in the passing on of their faith, by demonstrating a personal relationship with God as their most important responsibility as parents.

Laura reverently bowed her head and began to pray. The four children immediately began to pray along with her in unison. "Angel of God, my guardian dear, to whom God's love, commits me here. Ever this day, be at my side, to light and guard, to rule and guide. Lord, protect me from all harm and danger. In the name of the Father, and of the Son, and of the Holy Spirit, we pray, Amen."

So finally, the four children made their way through the kitchen door, as their mother kissed each of them on the cheek and blessed each one with the sign of the cross on their forehead.

"Irene, there is a big celebration this evening at the farmhouse. I will call you at school when I am ready for you. When you hear your mother's voice, come home immediately.

"Walk closely together, against the traffic, and stay to the side of the road. Cover every part of your body or you'll quickly get frostbitten."

Only after those maternal admonitions did Laura watch the four children disappear in the snow, beginning their journey up Gilbert Road toward the village, and then tightly closed the kitchen door. No sooner had Laura closed the door than it opened once more.

It was Irene. "I forgot my math book. It's right there on the table. I have my homework inside the book." She apologized to her mother.

"Jesus, Mary, and Joseph, Irene! Bless yourself immediately. It's bad luck to return for something you left behind. Here's your book. I'll want to see that corrected homework when you come home. Now go, be on your way and be careful."

Such superstitions were an undeniable part of the Irish culture, especially of those fondly known as the "Shanty Irish." The Shanty Irish were generally impoverished and possessed little formal education. However, they had a work ethic that stretched beyond the stratosphere and were extremely proud of their heritage. They also carried with them from the "old country" all the folklore that could frighten children and adults alike.

Laura's mother, Delia, reveled in her capacity to entertain an audience with stories that made the hairs on their necks stand on end, while sending children to bed sleepless, with their imaginations running wild at the sound of anything inside or outside the house. Inevitably, the children were discovered sharing beds. However, Laura remained quiet on such issues without ever contradicting her mother. She depended on her personal relationship with the Lord to guide her life, and knew better than to worry about the antics and fears of superstition. Although, after being raised by the likes of Delia Timothy her entire life, one could not blame Laura if she inadvertently let one slip past her lips. However, this folklore was definitely not something with which Laura wanted to indoctrinate her children.

The town of Ovid is a very small town, comprising only thirty-eight square acres of sprawling, rich, sparsely populated farmland. This is precisely why Europeans began to immigrate and settle in the town. They found a livelihood at farming and were not afraid of the hard work. The town was officially established in 1794. Among the immigrants were plenty of Roman Catholic Irish. In fact, the Irish Catholics were the third largest population followed only by the English and the Germans. A walk through the only Catholic cemetery in town, Holy Cross Cemetery on Gilbert Road, could make one believe they were in County Cork, Ireland instead of Ovid, New York as they read the names on the tombstones. However, no one knew better than Michael Corcoran, that the indigenous people of the area were the Iroquois Indians. As much as Delia Timothy loved to tell tales of Irish Folklore from the "old country," Michael Corcoran loved to tell tales of the Seneca Indians.

The Gilbert Home

Michael and Laura's homestead was at the end of Gilbert Road, at the intersection of Route 132 in the town of Ovid. It was a simple, white, two story house with a large yard surrounded by vast fields and woods. The home became affectionately known as the "Gilbert House" and was to be the birthplace of Laura's children. The Gilbert House was conveniently located, just a few miles down Route 132 from Leo's stone farmhouse. The farmhouse was a beautiful, large home on several acres of fertile land. It served as the gathering place for all the family festivities and holidays, including the weekly Sunday dinner; aunts, uncles, and cousins all attended. The farmhouse further provided a location for the cousins to work during the summer months when school was closed. Laura made certain her children understood the value of hard work. "An idle mind is the devil's workshop," Laura would remind her children if she heard even a whisper of complaint.

The Old Stone Farmhouse

Additionally, the house was located approximately two miles directly down Gilbert Road from Main Street in the village of Ovid. It was a small, very quaint, idyllic Main Street reminiscent of Mayberry, USA. There was a single, blinking light on Route 96A. If you missed that blinking light, you would miss Ovid entirely and likely end up in Ithaca, New York approximately thirty minutes later. However, if you attentively noticed that blinking light on

Route 96A and turned right, you would be on Main Street in the village of Ovid. It was a small village with a grocery store, a soda shop, a library, a fire station, a few homes, a small hotel, the only Catholic Church in town, Holy Cross, and Seneca County School. This was the school the Corcoran children walked to each morning, encompassing the entire stretch of Gilbert Road. There was little else to be found on Gilbert Road as it was mostly farmland and fields with the exception of Holy Cross Cemetery.

As the four older Corcoran children made their way up the stretch of Gilbert Road to the county school on Main Street in the village, they could hardly see or be seen. The wind was driving the snow across the barren fields creating whiteout conditions. They were thanking God that at least the piercing wind was at their backs and not slicing their tender, young faces like a razor blade. Glenn and Irene walked in front, Leo and Joyce were a mere half-step directly behind them. Glenn, Leo, and Joyce, raising their voices above the howling wind, were busy complaining about the weather conditions and the fact that schools rarely closed under such circumstances.

Irene was oblivious to the conversation. Her head was pointed down; chin securely nestled in her navy blue coat. The plaid scarf she had received for Christmas was tightly wrapped around her face. She removed herself from the conversation, not because she was immune to the cold; she simply did not understand the benefits of focusing on the storm. Instead, her mind drifted to summer, to her favorite time of the year, early July. She pictured the ditches along Gilbert Road filled with bundle upon bundle of the most beautiful, bright, orange, tiger lilies instead of the snow drifts. She envisioned the countless swarms of colorful butterflies busily floating from one flower to the next. She recalled how astonishingly beautiful the entire two mile stretch of Gilbert Road was during that time of the year.

Irene was convinced that Gilbert Road, during early July, was the most beautiful botanical garden in the world. She recalled the rich fragrance of the freshly tilled soil of the farmers' fields; fields replete with sprouts of various grains. There was barley, wheat, oats, and corn that was always "knee-high by the 4th of July." Irene could not help herself from remembering that July also welcomed the ripe, red cherries that were tiny, white blossoms on the branches of the trees just a couple of months earlier. She could readily identify a cherry tree by it's distinctive bark. She chuckled as she thought of how the family climbed those trees, in a race against flocks of birds, to pick the most ripened, plump, rich, red cherries. She recalled the amazed expression on her mother's face when they returned home with bags filled with the succulent fruit. Laura knew the children were expecting her to make a cherry pie from scratch.

Irene deliberately concentrated on looking forward to better days when she would be enjoying another of her mother's homemade cherry pies. It was absolutely her favorite pie. She recalled with uncanny detail, the memories of savoring her pie while sitting on the backyard picnic table in the early evening, while enjoying the spectacle of the fireflies. The fireflies flashed in the bushes and brush that surrounded the yard, causing it to look like a 4th of July celebration. Irene became so obsessed with her anticipation of July that, almost miraculously, the joy of understanding that better days were yet to come, served as an effective antidote to the bitter cold. She just continued to focus on the glory and joy of July that surely would come, and come soon. Irene was cognizant of just how fast life was passing and that this storm was merely an interruption of the promised joy yet to come. That was Irene's disposition; to always look forward to the better times yet to come. Undoubtedly, she acquired this disposition by heeding the wisdom shared by her astute mother.

Irene's comforting recollections and anticipations were suddenly interrupted when she heard Joyce loudly announce, "There! There are the gates to the main driveway into Holy Cross Cemetery." Joyce used her finger to point across the road. "Do you see them, Glenn? They're directly across the road. We're more than halfway to school. Thank God. My feet are so frozen I can't even feel them!" exclaimed Joyce.

Irene looked across the road, and through the blinding, drifting snow, she could see the tall gates to the center driveway of Holy Cross Cemetery. It is a relatively small country cemetery with only three driveways granting access; one driveway situated on each side of the gated main entrance. Irene began to think to herself how different the cemetery looked in mid-summer than it did on this blustery, winter day. In the summer, she considered the cemetery to be very beautiful. It had tall oak trees with branches reaching so high towards the blue sky that one would think those branches could touch the fluffy, white, cumulous clouds. There was one particular area in the cemetery that she thought was especially beautiful in the middle of summer. Irene began concentrating on this spot as she continued the second half of her march toward Main Street and Seneca County School in the midst of the fierce snowstorm.

Irene's favorite spot was located down the third driveway of the cemetery, almost to the end of the drive. There, looking to your right, you were afforded a panoramic view of Seneca Lake resting placidly at the bottom of the rolling countryside of farmland filled with grain and corn. Seneca Lake is one of the Finger Lakes; it happens to be the deepest of the Finger Lakes and therefore the coldest, even in July. On a sunny day, the cool waters of the lake had a distinctive, indigo hue that was breathtaking. From summer to summer, as Irene visited her favorite spot in the cemetery, she often thought to herself how quickly life was passing and how very little Ovid had changed over those quickly passing years.

There is an element of Irene's thoughts that still rings true to this day. One can still pull in the third driveway of Holy Cross Cemetery on Gilbert Road and venture to just about the end of the road. You can stand where Irene so often stood as a child, looking to the right, beholding the splendor of Seneca Lake. The oak trees are still there and more gigantic than before. The Gilbert House still stands on the corner of the end of Gilbert Road at the intersection of Route 132. The stone farmhouse stands more beautiful than ever. The single, blinking light still functions at the corner of Route 96A and Main Street in the village of Ovid. One visible difference would be that the rolling hillsides of grain and corn have, in many cases, been replaced by vineyards. In fact, Leo's old, stone farmhouse is surrounded by vineyards.

The most significant difference between the Ovid of that frigid, January morning of 1934 and the Ovid of today, is arguably not the replacement of farmland with vineyards. To capture and be transformed by the biggest change in this small, thirty-eight acre town, one would need to enter the third driveway of Holy Cross Cemetery, almost to the end of the drive, and look to the left instead of looking to the right towards the lake. There, you will see five grave markers; one of them inscribed "Irene."

It takes a discerning eye to read these five markers and realize that they each raise astonishing questions, serious questions, without giving even a hint of an answer. Carefully reading the five markers inevitably leaves one thinking, "Oh my goodness, what possibly could have happened here? What in God's name happened to this family?" It will send a chill, colder than the waters of Seneca Lake, up and down your spine.

Whatever happened to Irene? What happened to that innocent child filled with a zealous love of her parents, her ancestry, the beautiful countryside, and her ardent, vibrant faith? What happened to the summer dreams and fantasies that fill every young girl's heart, including hers? Little did that innocent child know that life would present her with incomprehensible challenges, much more severe than a mere two-mile walk to school in the frigid temperatures of winter with its knee-high snow.

Life would present Irene with challenges that would test her faith in a fiery crucible of unimaginable proportions. In that fiery crucible, innocence was lost forever and fortitude was formed. The singular relief she received in the furnace that so fiercely tested her faith was the promise, "For I know well the plans I have for you, plans to prosper you and not to harm you, plans to give you hope and a future" (Jeremiah

29:11). Irene leaned on those words, she depended on those words, she literally breathed those words daily for her survival. Most importantly, Irene believed those words, and in so doing, astounded countless people with a fortitude that most have never personally witnessed.

It all began in a tiny town named Ovid.

A wise person once said, "The same well that holds your capacity to experience genuine joy was dug by your sorrow and pain." Irene's well was deep. It also was filled to the brim with "rivers of the water of life" (Revelations 22:1). This story beckons you to drink from Irene's well and personally experience the miracle of genuine joy in the Lord. Whatever the unique circumstances of your personal life may be, your thirst shall be quenched. Irene's steadfast journey puts flesh and bones to the verse from Isaiah 54:17, "No weapon forged against you shall prevail." You will be transformed as Irene has transformed Ovid, New York forever by arguably becoming one of its greatest saints!

Irene's parents: Michael and Laura Mae Corcoran

Chapter Two

FOR BETTER OR FOR WORSE

It was exactly 11:30 a.m. on Saturday, September 14, 1946, a pleasant autumn day filled with sunshine, bright blue skies, and moderate temperatures in the mid-sixties. The foliage was at near peak. As the sun reflected off the deep reds and golds of the maple trees, it made each tree look as colorful as a Christmas tree adorned with an array of spectacular lights. In no uncertain terms, it was a phenomenally, beautiful autumn day. All the prayers for the perfect weather had obviously not gone unheeded.

Michael Corcoran was nervously pacing the floor of the vestibule of Immaculate Conception Church, in Ithaca, New York. Dressed in a black tuxedo with a grey tie, Michael looked extremely handsome despite his constant complaints of feeling so uncomfortable wearing formal attire. Michael had always been a rather mildly, anxious man. He certainly earned his reputation as being an early riser and was even better known as an early arriver.

Michael stole another moment to admire the gold watch that Irene had presented him with earlier that morning as a pre-birthday gift. His actual birthday was September 29th, approximately two weeks away. Michael was born on the Feast of St. Michael the Archangel, therefore, he was extremely proud of what he considered to be a strong name. With tears welling up in the eyes of this strong, proud man, Michael once again gently rubbed his thumb over the inscription on the back of the gold watch: "To Dad, with all my love, Irene." As he continued to caress the watch, he became overwhelmed by how fast time seemed to have passed. It was absolutely astounding to Michael that today, in less than thirty minutes, he would be giving Irene's hand away in marriage.

Michael pondered how much he would miss his daughter around their home in Ithaca. After all, Irene had always been such a charming and obedient daughter, even as a little girl. She was always a delight to have around the house. Michael fondly remembered the day Irene was born in the Gilbert House in Ovid as vividly as if it were yesterday. Ever since that memorable, joyous day, Irene remained the "apple of her father's eye." Where had the time gone? How could years have passed as if they were hours, weeks as if they had been minutes, days as though they were seconds?

Michael recalled memory upon memory of how Irene demonstrated such heartfelt affection for her parents, especially her mother. She had always been a living example of the commandment "Honor Thy Father and Thy Mother," Michael thought to himself. Irene dutifully completed her schoolwork without prodding and often received sincere, warm compliments from her teachers. Besides her schoolwork, Michael recalled what a tremendous help she consistently was to her mother. He could envision her helping his wife for hours, preparing, serving, and cleaning up after every family meal. He could clearly picture in his mind, Irene standing in front of the large farmer's sink, scrubbing the pots and pans. She assisted with the laundry too and Michael grinned, recalling how Irene had to use all her weight and strength to turn the handle on the wooden wringer atop the old, noisy washer. Michael utilized a cleanly pressed handkerchief to wipe the tears streaming down his cheeks.

He recalled the countless times he would sweep Irene up in the air, squeezing her firmly with both his strong arms, to assist her as she quickly fastened dozens of wooden clothespins to hang the laundry on the line that stretched the length of the backyard. When the laundry had dried in the warm sun and gentle breeze, Irene helped her mother collect the clothes in a large, woven, laundry basket. Then she lent a hand with the ironing of what seemed to be enough clothes to fill every drawer and closet in the house. When something needed stitching, she either threaded the needle for her mother or did the sewing herself. Michael just could not have been prouder of his daughter, Irene. His heart was bursting with well wishes for the one he came to love so dearly and respect so deeply. *Irene deserves nothing but the best in life, nothing but the very best for my little girl.*

Michael was so deep in thought that he was inattentive to the dozens of guests making their way up the stairs, through the vestibule, and into the church. However, his fond reflections of the fast-paced passing of decades of memories he would forever cherish in the deepest recesses of his heart, were abruptly interrupted when he glanced once again at his new watch and discovered it was already 11:45 a.m. The bride and the mother-of-the-bride were nowhere to be seen. These were precisely the things that made Michael Corcoran a nervous man. After all, he must have admonished all the ladies to be sure they arrived at the vestibule of the church not a minute later than 11:30 a.m. Michael was certain these were his last words to the ladies as he departed for the church at 10:30 a.m., a full ninety minutes before the scheduled start of the wedding ceremony. Michael too often felt a deep compunction that he needed to be the first to arrive at any event, and thus be in a position to monitor everything to assure all was going well. Today, more than any other day, he wanted a perfect, flawless ceremony for the daughter he loved so dearly.

Both Michael and Laura were thrilled with Irene's choice for a husband. He definitely was the answer to her parent's most fervent prayers for their children; a decent, devoted, and spiritual spouse. He was a handsome Irishman; his name was Richard William O'Brien II. Richard grew up in Ithaca, New York on North Aurora Street. The house was located at the base of the extremely steep hill leading up to the University of Cornell. The campus afforded a splendid view of the city of Ithaca and Cayuga Lake, especially from the top of the bell tower, for those daring enough to climb the circular staircase in the center of the tower. Cayuga is another of the Finger Lakes. Richard, or Dick, as his Ithaca friends and three sisters called him, was himself a graduate of the University of Cornell. Richard William O'Brien II was also a proud veteran of the United States Air Force and served in active combat during World War II. Yes, both Laura and Michael were very confident that Irene's future would be a secure and happy one with the likes of Dick O'Brien.

Dick O'Brien, U.S. Air Force

Dick's father was an immigrant from Ireland with a brogue so strong it was, at times, difficult to understand what he was saying. Unlike the Corcorans and the Fitzsimons, the O'Briens were not part of the clan that fondly came to be known as the Shanty Irish. Rather, they were considered to be what some have called the Lace Curtain Irish. These distinctions were ascribed to the Irish in the United States; they did not exist in the homeland of Ireland. The Lace Curtain Irish, in contrast to the Shanty Irish, tended to be a little more economically secure and a bit more educated. Further, the Lace Curtain Irish were not as steeped in the folklore that certainly was at the heart of simple folks like Delia Timothy Fitzsimons. Make no mistake, the Lace Curtain Irish were every bit as proud to be Irish as anyone who immigrated from the Emerald Isle. After all, they had suffered terrible persecution in their homeland and were more often than not, discriminated against upon their arrival in the United States. "Irish Need Not Apply" was a signage found in more than one business establishment.

The O'Brien house on North Aurora Street was a mammoth, double, three-story house. The O'Briens lived in one-half of the "mansion," providing a large living room, large dining room, fully equipped kitchen, and four bedrooms and a bath upstairs; a fifth bedroom was situated on the third floor. Additionally, there was a basement apartment with a private entrance from outdoors. There were perfectly pressed, white lace curtains adorning all the windows, both downstairs and upstairs. The kitchen table did not wobble, nor was it the only table in the house. The dining room table was part of an exquisite, cherry, dining room set, with a matching cabinet to display all the beautiful china. Fresh flowers were usually set at the center of the dining room table. There was a silver tea set proudly displayed on its own stand that received regular polishing from Theresa, Dick's mother. Beautiful antiques accessorized the entire house. There was a huge grandfather clock in the entrance hallway just at the bottom of the stairs.

The other half of the house was partitioned to provide four apartments, as well as an additional fifth basement apartment. The apartments were always occupied and provided additional income. Soon, one of those apartments would become the first home of the newlyweds.

The stories shared within the confines of this house on North Aurora were not exactly the hair-raising, heart-stopping, stories of the Irish banshees, relayed by Delia Fitzsimons that sent her grandchildren scurrying into a single bed. Rather, in this house, you were likely to hear Theresa O'Brien, with her unmistakable, distinguished Bostonian accent, fondly and formally recounting her stories of growing up in Boston and spending summers in Hyannis Port, Massachusetts. She would sit in her favorite, wooden, rocking chair next to the front window, place her hands on her lap, sweetly twiddle her thumbs ever so slowly, and tell colorful and captivating stories. She could relate, with remarkable detail, the scene of the Kennedy family arriving at Sunday Mass in the white horse-drawn carriage, and the attire everyone wore to church. She had nothing but superlative comments for how well Joseph and Rose Kennedy raised their children to be so obedient and well-behaved in church.

On the surface, it may seem like the bride and groom came from separate worlds and shared little in common.

Nothing could be further from the truth. Both Richard and Irene, in addition to sharing an Irish ancestry, shared a firm, reverent, personal, devotion to the Lord as their Savior. They were children that genuinely honored their parents, even as adults and they shared strikingly similar values on what was important in life. Both were deeply in love with each other; nothing else mattered. Richard and Irene were most certainly destined for an ecstatically happy future!

Richard W. O'Brien and Theresa O'Brien with Dick

At precisely 11:55 a.m., Irene and her mother finally arrived at the church. They were greeted by an extremely nervous father-of-the-bride who immediately whisked both of them into a small room adjacent to the vestibule. "Jesus, Mary, and Joseph! Where have you been? The ceremony is scheduled to begin in five minutes. Didn't I tell you to be here not a minute later than 11:30?"

"Please, Michael. Not now; not today," replied a very nervous and excited Laura.

"Everything is just fine, Dad," Irene assured him as she gave her dad a huge, long hug. "I'm going to need you to be calm as you walk me down the aisle, Dad. Lord knows, I'm nervous enough!"

Irene's brother, Glenn, interrupted the conversation just as it was beginning with a light knock on the door. "Mom, are you ready? It's time for me to walk you down the aisle. Everyone has been seated."

Laura looked beautiful in her simple, navy blue dress with a white collar, matching navy heels, a navy hat, and white gloves that extended to her elbows. Any shade of blue seemed to be Laura's favorite choice of fabric as it stood in contrast to her beautiful, silver-white hair. It is not an uncommon trait for the Irish to have their hair turn white at a relatively young age.

"Yes, Glenn, I'm all set." Laura gave Irene a kiss on the cheek as an expression of her deep love and then quickly wiped off the lipstick impression of the kiss with a tissue in hand. "Oh, Mom, I love you so much," Irene replied, as she pulled her mother toward her in a firm embrace. Tears rolled down both their cheeks as Glenn opened the door and took his mother by the arm.

Suddenly, the pipe organ in the choir loft opened up with such vibrato in its chords that the door to the small room holding Irene and her father, shook. Michael took a final look at his new watch and it was precisely noon. Michael felt both a sense of pride and a sense of relief that he had done such a superb job in arriving early to the church and organizing all the intricate details like a fine, Swiss watch.

"Dad, that's our cue! Are we ready for this?" inquired a nervous Irene. Taking one last glance in the large mirror, Irene asked, "How do I look, Dad?"

As Michael grabbed his daughter by the hand and slipped it through his bent arm, he leaned over and whispered in her ear, "You look as beautiful as an angel that just fell from heaven, my darling."

Irene smiled and nervously took her place in the back of the church, with her arm tightly intertwined with her father's and her head resting ever so lightly on his shoulder. Irene could feel every eye gazing upon her as the congregation turned their heads to the back of the church. A gasp could be heard, even above the loud chords of the organ, as the invited guests caught their first glimpse of the bride.

Irene looked absolutely stunning! Standing there in an ivory, satin dress with a short train, she looked like royalty. Even through the veil covering her face, you could not help but notice her beautiful, naturally wavy, black hair. Those blue Irish eyes were smiling like they had never smiled before. They sparkled more brilliantly than the waters of Seneca Lake on a sunny day and they seemed to beckon you to dive right into them for a swim. Everyone had always conceded that Irene was a beautiful woman, but she never looked more radiant than she did this day. This was because, as Irene looked down the long church aisle at Richard O'Brien, it was clear she was a woman deeply in love.

Michael needed to assist his nervous daughter with her first few steps on this wonderful journey toward a new life. Soon, Irene began acknowledging those in attendance with her dazzling smile and a nod of her head while several guests were wiping away tears of sheer joy for their wonderful friend. She could read in the adoring eyes of her guests, the love and best wishes each conveyed for genuine happiness. That walk down the church aisle seemed as long to Irene as the walk from the Gilbert House to the school on Main Street in the village of Ovid. *Good Lord, how quickly time has passed. It seems like just yesterday I was making that daily journey down Gilbert Road to school.*

As Irene continued her slow pace down the long church aisle, she filled her mind with the dreams of sharing her life with the man she loved so deeply. Her head was spinning. She dreamed of the house she would share someday with her new husband. It would have to be a large house because Irene wanted a large family. It should have a big yard for the children to play in. Children! Irene anticipated with joy the day she and Richard would welcome their first child. She couldn't fathom how joyful that experience would be. To be a mother! Would it be a boy or a girl? It didn't really matter, there would be many more to come. All that truly mattered to her, the single most important concern of her heart, was that each and every one of her children be born healthy and strong. This was Irene's most ardent prayer to the Lord.

As she concentrated her gaze upon Richard standing at the front of the aisle, she thought to herself how incredibly handsome he looked in his formal attire. She dreamed of the first Christmas they would share together as husband and wife in a few short months. Irene had promised herself to make Christmas a spiritual, joyful, and memorable occasion for her many children, just as her mother had done for them. Her mind was running a mile a minute with dreams of a bright, happy future, shared with the man whom she loved more than any other human being. Then, the daydreaming came to an abrupt end, as Michael firmly shook Richard's hand, and gave away the hand of the daughter he had so fervently loved for twenty-six years. Irene watched with a careful eye as Michael joined Laura in the front pew, and then gave the Lord heartfelt thanks for blessing her with two such beautiful, spiritual parents. She prayed that she and Richard could live up to their standards as parents.

Finally, the time came to exchange vows. Richard and Irene held hands and did not take their eyes off each other. There, in Immaculate Conception Church, in the presence of God, their parents, relatives, and friends, Richard and Irene publicly declared their eternal love for each other. "For better or for worse, in good times and in bad times, till death do us part."

At last, the official words issued from the priest's lips, "I now pronounce you, man and wife. What God has joined together, let no man put asunder."

That little girl from Ovid, that country girl who was born in the Gilbert Road House, the girl who spent summers working hard on her uncle's farm, the obedient child who had no limits to her love, devotion, and service to her parents, was now Mrs. Richard William O'Brien.

People feasted at the reception that followed, because in those days, Catholics fasted the entire day before receiving Communion. There was dancing, laughing, and chatter among old friends. All the traditional ceremonies for a wedding reception were included. It did not matter whether you were Shanty Irish or Lace Curtain Irish. Irene never looked more joyous or more radiantly in love. Finally, her dreams were being realized and that certainly was worth celebrating.

A brief honeymoon in Lake George, situated in the lower mountains of Adirondack State Park, followed all the festivities of the perfectly executed wedding and the celebratory reception. Upon their return to Ithaca, the newlyweds met with their parents and began the process of selecting photographs to compile an album. Irene loved pouring over the photos with her mother, making the difficult decision of which to select as a permanent keepsake. These photographs represented the beginning of what she had dreamed of for years. Irene was amazed at how unbelievably quickly the years had passed. The photographs were evidence that her dreams indeed had come true. Discretion was exercised in making the final selections, because the official, final product would represent the cornerstone upon which Irene and Richard would build their future together in the Lord.

Irene's Wedding Day

It delighted Laura to see her daughter so ecstatically happy. Irene kept no secrets about her desire to start a family. Laura reminded her daughter that whether she had girls, boys, or twins, was of little consequence; the only important thing was that all the children be born healthy. Indeed, this was the shared consensus of Irene and Richard whenever they discussed their philosophy of parenting. Husband and wife were firm in their resolve that their most important responsibility was to raise a family with a deep, personal devotion to the Lord Jesus and to the Church.

It did not take long for Richard and Irene's dream of becoming parents to unfold. In early August 1947, Irene's prayer for a healthy baby was answered as she gave birth to a baby girl. Richard and Irene were overwhelmed with joy as they welcomed Sharon Ann and officially became a family. Irene could not fathom how she could be happier!

Sharon was just a year old when Irene discovered she was once again pregnant. Prayers for a healthy child commenced immediately. Laura visited church frequently and prayed fervently for this intention. Once again, it was in early August that Irene delivered her second daughter. Richard and Irene selected the name Cassie Marie for their newborn. The couple laughed with delight as they realized they had doubled the size of their family in two years. Both Richard and Irene expressed their gratitude to the Lord for another, sweet, adorable, healthy baby girl. The responsibility of caring for two babies was exhausting to be sure, but Irene was elated.

An employment opportunity for Richard took the family temporarily to Norristown, Pennsylvania. Irene once again was informed that she was pregnant. Richard's colleagues at work teased him that with two daughters, it was time for a son! He could not argue with them. He thought it would be wonderful to have a son, but in the deepest recesses of his heart, he recognized the reality that the most important issue was the health of his wife and newborn baby.

On Columbus Day, 1950, Richard received his first son. Irene and Richard were ecstatic! Theresa celebrated with her son, and suggested the baby boy be named Christopher, since he was born on Columbus Day. However, there was not any discussion or hesitation on the part of Richard in selecting a name for his first-born son. The baby would be named Richard William O'Brien III. This son was to become his namesake and would pass the name on to another generation. Richard could not have been prouder. Richard William O'Brien III would come to be known as "Ricky" by his siblings and friends.

Unbelievably, Ricky was just two months old when Irene, once again, discovered she was pregnant. Richard and Irene conceded that raising three young babies was indeed a chore, but their exhaustion did not dampen the excitement they shared over the anticipation of receiving a new addition to the O'Brien family. A move returning to Ithaca was completed in time to welcome a second, healthy, son in late September 1951. Because the newborn was delivered so close to her father's birthday, Irene insisted that this child would honor her father by bestowing upon him the name, Michael Joseph. Irene's father could not have been more delighted and honored.

Dick's colleagues teased him relentlessly. "My goodness, you have four babies at home, two of them less than a year old. You have four children; half of them are girls, half of them are boys. What could be more perfect than that?

Enough!" Dick laughed, but he understood that he and his wife had agreed they would accept any and all children the good Lord decided to bless them with. Dick suspected that eventually, more children would be on the way.

Dick was seldom wrong. In less than two years, they were expecting their fifth child. The couple was delighted. This was Irene's dream for a large family being actualized. From the time she was a little country girl in Ovid, New York, until the day she walked down that aisle so naively in Immaculate Conception Church, Irene dreamed of nothing more intently than she did of having a large, Irish family. She found great delight in the family they were becoming and she immensely enjoyed the responsibility of being a mother. Irene looked forward to welcoming a new member to the expanding O'Brien family.

Still residing in Ithaca, Irene went into labor with her fifth child on the scorching, hot day of July 1, 1953. July had always been Irene's favorite month. En route to the hospital, she thought of how the tiger lilies along Gilbert Road must be in full bloom. The fireflies surely would be brightening the evenings in the bushes and brush in the backyard of the old Gilbert House. The cherries would be ripe for picking from the multitude of trees sprawling across the rolling hillsides of Route 132. The corn must already be knee high in the farmer's fields. Irene considered all these things to be favorable signs from the Lord that her newest child would be as healthy and strong as her other four children.

In the throes of labor, Dr. Phillips dutifully kept encouraging Irene to "push." Irene was comfortable with Dr. Phillips because he was the doctor that delivered her other three children that were born in Ithaca. Irene had acquired a confidence in his competence. At last, the loud cry of the newborn baby was a symphony of sweet music to Irene's ears. She lay there exhausted, looking down at Dr. Phillips' face. Irene noticed a perplexing look on the doctor's face and could not help but be aware that he was eerily silent. The doctor hadn't even announced whether the baby was a girl or a boy.

Sensing the panic rising in her heart, Irene exclaimed, "Doctor! What is it? Doctor, talk to me! Is there something wrong with my baby? Is it a boy or a girl? Doctor, I want to see my baby right this instant!"

As the baby was being cleaned and gently wrapped, Dr. Phillips fumbled for words and motioned for the nurse to bring the husband in immediately.

"Is it a boy or a girl?" Irene inquired once again, this time with an authoritative tone that sounded more like a Pontiff speaking ex-cathedra. It seemed obvious to her that the baby's gender was not an issue, but that something was seriously wrong; she felt her heart painfully crushing inside her chest.

As Richard entered the delivery room fully masked, Dr. Phillips finally announced, "It's a boy." His tone, however, lacked the enthusiasm a parent would come to expect from the doctor.

Irene forced herself to sit up in her bed. "Doctor! I'm not asking again, is there a problem? Bring my child to me immediately!" Her voice could be heard echoing down the hospital corridors; it was a most pathetic cry of dismay and panic, sounding like a wounded animal in a cage.

Before handing the newborn child to his parents, Dr. Phillips reluctantly and empathetically stated, "Yes, we have a problem here. I'm compelled to acknowledge, that personally, I've never seen this condition in my career. I'll do my best to explain the complex intricacies of the situation, then I'll have a colleague from the University of Cornell confirm my diagnosis later today."

"What?!" Irene exclaimed. With a pathetic, heartbreaking sob, she demanded, "Dr. Phillips, let me see my baby, please!"

Irene feared what she was about to discover about her fifth child. Richard immediately moved to his wife's bedside and took a firm grasp of her hand; he felt the sweat on her hand and noticed the sweat on her brow. He leaned over and kissed his wife on the cheek and wiped her brow.

"Your child has an extremely rare skin condition," Dr. Phillips informed the parents. "I must advise you before I place the newborn in your arms, that it's extremely critical that you handle the baby very gingerly; even hugging the baby could do irreparable, further damage to the skin."

Dr. Phillips then carefully and gingerly placed the baby in Irene's extended arms, with Richard intently looking on. Irene carefully examined her baby's face. The only exposed skin was the face; the rest of the skin was covered with sterile gauze and wrapped in a soft blanket. All Irene could do was stare deeply into the newborn's innocent, blue eyes, that had the longest black lashes she had ever seen. She quickly noticed the blisters and sores on portions of the baby's face and head.

Irene began to sob inconsolably as she looked up at Richard and said, "The poor child looks almost as if he's been burned."

Suddenly, Irene began shaking and wailing like an Irish banshee. "Dr. Phillips, I implore you, please tell me my child is going to heal and is going to live! Help us, dear Lord, I beg of you, please help us. I promise I will do anything, absolutely anything you ask of me Lord, just heal my innocent child." Irene's heartfelt cries reverberated throughout the room. Tears were rolling down the face of Dr. Phillips.

Irene had never been so distraught in her entire life. She had to bravely refrain from hugging her newborn child and smothering him with kisses, when that was precisely what her maternal instincts were demanding that she do. She wanted to whisper in her baby's ear and promise, "This will soon all go away," but Irene could do none of that. Nothing had been so painful to her in her entire life. She felt as though seven swords had pierced her heart.

Reluctantly, Dr. Phillips said, in a compassionate, whispered tone, "I must remove the baby now so that he can be further treated."

"Oh, please, Doctor, just one more minute before you take him away," Irene sighed. She took a final look at those beautiful, blue eyes with the long lashes. "Those eyes are indisputably the most beautiful eyes I have ever seen," Irene sighed.

She sneaked one gentle kiss on her baby's forehead. She then carefully lifted her arms, as if she were surrendering to the authorities, and allowed Dr. Phillips to take her baby from her.

Irene felt like Jesus in Gethsemane. In an audible whisper, Richard listened as his wife prayed, "Father, if it be possible, let this cup pass from me; yet not my will, but Thy will be done" (Luke 22:42).

Irene recounted the many years of attending church during Holy Week from the time she was a little girl; listening intently to the reading of the Passion of her Lord and Savior; recalling how deeply disturbing it was to her, listening particularly to the verse, "My soul is deeply grieved, to the point of death" (Matthew 26:38). She always considered this to be the most poignant verse in the entire bible, and responded to those specific words with compassion and gratitude to her Savior. She viewed the verse as epitomizing the unimaginable pain her Lord endured, to the point of causing Him to sweat blood.

Now, this verse took on a deeper significance for Irene as she lay in her hospital bed, contemplating the mysteries of her faith. Never before had Irene felt more empathy for her Savior during His agonizing night in the Garden, than she did this day as she lay in that bed. If Irene had any consolation at all, it was an assurance that the Lord understood her emotions and had compassion on her; He suffered with her. *My soul is also deeply grieved to the point of death. Have mercy on your humble servant, oh Lord. Please be my strength and salvation.*

Dr. Phillips excused himself, taking the baby with him, promising to return shortly. Richard firmly held onto his wife's hand. "Oh, Richard, what are we going to do?" Irene questioned in desperation.

Richard responded, "I can't honestly say, Honey. We need to wait for Dr. Phillips to return." Then he softly took hold of his wife's chin and turned her face toward him so he could look directly in her eyes. "In our marriage vows, we promised to love each other and to be with each other 'For better or worse, in good times and in bad times.' I promise you, Irene, I will be with you every step of this journey, no matter in what direction this journey takes us. You shall not walk alone." Richard watched tears streaming down his wife's cheeks, and affectionately wiped them dry with his hand.

"But Dick, did you ever think the day we made those vows, that it would ever come to this?" Irene inquired rhetorically. "I just remember being so in love, dreaming of happily raising a large family of healthy children. I was so naive!" she lamented.

"You're exhausted and you need to try to rest until Dr. Phillips returns," Richard encouraged Irene. "I'm here with you, for better or worse. Let's just wait to see what the doctor has to say. I love you, Irene. Please try to rest."

Richard pulled his chair so that he could be closer to his wife. He did a valiant job ignoring his own feelings and concentrated solely on the despair his wife was suffering.

Irene lay motionless in her hospital bed, feeling numb and in a state of shock. She could hear the busy traffic outside her hospital bedroom through the open window, but she felt isolated from the rest of the world because her world seemed to have just been shattered. She heard conversations filled with jovial laughter down the corridor, and wondered if she would ever possess the capacity to laugh again. In the silence of her thoughts, she asked God a million and one questions. She received no answers - just silence. It was the most dreadful silence Irene had ever experienced. It enveloped her like a cold, wet blanket. Her heart was shattered into a million pieces. *And all the king's horses, and all the king's men, couldn't put 'Irene' together again.*

She finally opened her eyes and looked at Richard. "John, John Vincent, that's what we're naming this baby."

"That's a perfect name," Richard quickly concurred with his wife, "it sounds like a good, strong name."

"Yes, it does," agreed Irene, "but I fear we are the ones who will also need to be strong, and by God's grace we shall be."

Irene requested that Richard summon her mother, Laura. "I would like her present when Dr. Phillips returns." Richard immediately complied.

Chapter Three

GIVE US THIS DAY, OUR DAILY BREAD

Dr. Phillips' colleague from the University of Cornell confirmed John's diagnosis.

"There's just no easy way to present this information to the parents," Dr. Phillips sighed to his colleague. "It's such devastating news, and such an extremely rare disease that we know so little about. There aren't even any support groups that I could recommend to the parents, the condition is so rare. The rarity of the condition also precludes sufficient funding from being available for much needed research. There are more questions than there are answers concerning this rare condition."

"I certainly don't envy you having to inform the parents," added the colleague. "Would you like me to accompany you?"

"Thank you for the offer. I know the O'Briens well. I think another body in the room may just become a source of further panic," Dr. Phillips graciously responded.

Dr. Phillips walked the long hospital corridor slowly, as if he were procrastinating the inevitable experience of his dialogue with the O'Briens. He knew them to be such a happy couple and often commended them on the fine job they were doing raising their other four children. *This is the most difficult task I've ever faced in my career, I must be compassionate and professional.*

Dr. Phillips knocked on Irene's door and slowly entered the room. He greeted Irene, Richard, and Laura. The first thing Irene noticed about the doctor as he entered the room was that he looked as though someone had turned the lights off in his eyes. They appeared dark, hallow and filled with pain. Irene began to feel her heart race and pound within her chest. She squeezed Richard's hand firmly with her left hand, and her mother's hand tightly with her right hand.

"Is my baby going to live, Doctor? Please tell me that my baby will heal. Please tell me you have a treatment, some medicine, anything that will heal my baby!" Irene blurted out, unable to contain the panic in her heart. "You're a good and knowledgeable doctor. I know you must have something for my baby. Please tell me everything will be fine. I've always implicitly trusted you. Help me, Dr. Phillips. I beg of you!" Irene moaned with heart wrenching anguish. Dr. Phillips thought to himself, "I have never witnessed a more pathetic scene in my career!"

"Let's take this one step at a time, shall we?" suggested Dr. Phillips.

"Yes, certainly, Doctor, we'll do our best," assured Richard. "This moment has been weighing heavily upon our hearts, as I'm sure you can understand."

"I most certainly understand, and it's weighed on my heart also," assured Dr. Phillips. "Your baby has been born…"

"My 'baby' has a name," interrupted Irene. "His name is John! Please refer to him as John," insisted a sorrowing Irene, who naively sensed that calling the baby by his name would promise him a future.

"I apologize, Irene," responded Dr. Phillips with a tone of deep empathy in his voice. " I love the name you've selected," he added a little nervously. "John has been born with a form of an extremely rare congenital disease called epidermolysis bullosa, or EB for short. We know very little about this disease, but I'll do my very best to explain all that we've come to learn up to this point in time."

Dr. Phillips looked at the faces of Richard, Irene, and Laura, to acquire a sense of their readiness for him to continue. They all had their eyes intently fixed upon his. "We do know there are three distinct forms of the disease, EB. Including all three of these forms of this disease, only about six out of a million babies are born with EB. That gives you an idea of the extreme rarity of the disease."

"Stop!" screeched Irene. "Doctor, surely this can't be true regarding my John. Oh, my sweet Lord and Savior Jesus, please help me," Irene cried in desperation. "Mom, could you please get me a glass of water. I feel as though I'm going to faint!" A light-headed Laura, whose heart was also racing in her chest, immediately sprung up from her chair to retrieve a glass of water for the suffering inflaming her daughter's heart. Irene quickly emptied the glass of cold water and requested a second. Laura then returned to her chair, taking a firm hold of her daughter's hand.

"Would you prefer I return at a more suitable time?" inquired a compassionate Dr. Phillips. "Perhaps in a couple of hours?" he suggested.

"No, please continue, Doctor," insisted Richard, "delaying the news will only cause further anguish. Please continue."

"The specific type of EB that your baby, I'm sorry, the specific type of EB that John has been born with is called dystrophic epidermolysis bullosa or DEB for short. This is a more serious form of EB. Further, within the spectrum of patients born with DEB, patients can range from less severe symptoms of the disease to more extreme symptoms of the disease. John has been born with a more severe form of DEB, and virtually only one baby in a million is born with this more complicated form of DEB."

Dr. Phillips glanced at Irene and she looked as white as a sheet. He paused briefly before continuing, allowing her to catch her breath. He noticed that Laura was not looking at him, rather, her eyes were fixed on Irene, monitoring her every reaction as any loving mother would do.

"We have come to this conclusion because, upon carefully examining John, there are signs of blisters affecting the mucous membranes lining the mouth, and the throat, also. In all probability, the digestive tract is included. As these blister heal, they'll form scars. This cycle will make it increasingly difficult, sometimes painful, for John to eat, swallow, and excrete food."

Irene's ears were locked on every word emanating from the doctor's mouth. However, this all seemed so surreal to her, that Dr. Phillips' voice sounded like someone on the other end of a long-distance telephone call filled with static. As Laura continued to fix her eyes on the pain crippling Irene's face, she felt a bit like Mary, the mother of Jesus, watching her son suffer on the cross. Laura's heart was breaking, the likes of which she had never experienced. However, she knew she had to remain strong for the daughter she so deeply cherished.

Dr. Phillips continued cautiously, never taking his eyes off Irene. "The human skin consists of two layers. The outermost layer is called the epidermis and the layer underneath is called the dermis. In individuals with healthy skin, there are protein anchors between these two layers of skin that prevent the them from moving independently from each other, or shearing, as we sometimes call it. In babies like John, the two layers of skin lack the protein anchors that hold them together, resulting in extremely fragile skin. Some have compared the fragility of the skin to a butterfly's wing. Even only minor friction, like rubbing, pressure, or any sort of trauma, will separate the layers of skin and form blisters and painful sores. Once again, if these blisters and sores heal, and some may not, they will form painful scars."

Irene squeezed her mother's hand firmly, just the way she did whenever she was frightened as a child in the Gilbert House. She wished this was only a bad dream, but she understood it couldn't be, because even in her wildest imagination, she could never have conceived such a predicament. This was no dream, not even a nightmare, it was a stark reality that somehow she would have to embrace. This was asking a lot from a mere mortal human being, especially one who had previously filled her heart, since the time she was a little girl, with the dreams of being happily married with a large, healthy family.

Dr. Phillips was pained as he read the expressions on Richard, Irene, and Laura's faces. Feeling the need to be seated, Dr. Phillips pulled up a chair and seated himself before being able to continue with this most dreadful news.

"Additional complications of the progressive scarring can include fusion of the fingers, toes, and even the underarms. It will eventually cause extreme joint deformation, contraction of the knees, elbows, hands, and feet that will severely restrict movement, and will eventually make it impossible for John to walk, if he survives that long. This complication is likely to cause extreme disfigurement of the body.

"There will be frequent eye inflammations that cannot be treated with drops. Exposure to any source of light during these periods will cause extreme pain. Therefore, the eyes would need to be completely covered. The inflammation can linger for days, even beyond a week. Most unfortunately, should both eyes simultaneously become inflamed, John will be blind until the inflammation retreats in one or both eyes.

"There will be frequent anemia from the constant bleeding of the sores, eventually causing monthly hospital stays for blood transfusions. It will look as though portions of John's body, particularly his back, is covered with third-degree burns, making it uncomfortable for him to sit or lay down. The lesions will itch throughout most of the day and night. As a complication of the chronic skin damage, John will have an increased risk of developing skin cancer, particularly squamous cell carcinoma."

The room remained absolutely silent. To say that Richard, Irene, and Laura were stunned would be a gross understatement. This information was so shrouded in mystery, and the experience was so foreign to anything they could ever have imagined, that they did not even know what questions to ask Dr. Phillips. They just listened attentively in disbelief and without interruption. Irene kept foremost in her mind those beautiful, innocent, blue eyes with the long lashes that would surely look to her someday to explain the mystery of his suffering. Irene could not fathom where she would begin! What words could she ever find to satisfactorily explain his predicament, if he survived long enough to ask her questions? Those innocent, blue eyes were just indelibly seared in the mind of Irene.

Dr. Phillips continued his dissertation, "Management of the disease is a very intricate and time-consuming process and frankly speaking, a very difficult one to witness. In an attempt to prevent further abrasions to the skin, John will, much of the time, need to have his arms restrained to his crib. It's indeed a heart-wrenching sight to behold, but it's necessary to assist in an attempt to prevent further abrasions which would only add to John's suffering. His body will need to be gently washed with a prescription soap and rinsed thoroughly at least once daily.

"Careful wound care is critical. I cannot stress this enough. The wounds must be covered with strips of sterile gauze that have been coated with Vaseline. The Vaseline needs to be sterilized by baking the strips of coated gauze in an oven. Additional protective padding of the skin must be applied. The protective coating and the gauze will need to be removed daily for the skin to be cleansed as the process repeats itself. Mind you, this is a very time-consuming process easily taking hours to complete. Unfortunately, it will be excruciatingly painful for John, but the process is required.

"As the blistering and subsequent scaring continue to spread about John's body, it will be critical to keep him in a cool, temperature-controlled environment to prevent dehydration and excessive itching. I know that you'd like me to divulge a life expectancy. However, that is very difficult due to the rarity of the disease. The sparse data that we've collected at this point in time, indicates that most patients with this most severe form of DEB, have died at a very young age. I must tell you, due to the constrictions of the joints and the extreme disfigurement of the body, he will never resemble his true chronological age. He will never look, to an innocent bystander, to be any older than a child.

"I have several competent colleagues investigating an appropriate institution that will provide the extensive care required for John. I've emphasized the need to identify such an institution locally, so that you will be able to visit him."

"What?!" blurted Irene, in a tone that could have raised the dead, in firm protest to the suggestion of institutionalizing her new baby. "What are you saying, Dr. Phillips? Are you suggesting that John won't be coming home with me?"

Dr. Phillips immediately and calmly intervened, "Irene, John will require extremely skilled care. The care will be very demanding of one's time. It'll be challenging even for a trained, skilled, professional. Think of your other four children. Raising four children is, of itself, very demanding. You can't possibly properly care for John, understanding his condition will only worsen year after year, with four other children at home. Let's be reasonable, Irene, you have the other four children to think of, not to mention consideration of your own well-being."

"Never!" wailed Irene repeatedly with relentless sobs.

As she wiped her nose with a tissue quickly handed to her by Richard, Irene continued to vehemently protest any suggestion that John would be taken from her loving arms.

"I'll never institutionalize John! Doctor, you keep mentioning all the intricate care that will be required for John's survival. However, you neglect to mention the most important issue; the care John will need for his eternal survival. John will come home and experience the blessing of what it means to be part of a loving, Christian family, just as much as my other four children have been blessed. In the context of a loving, Christian family, John will come to personally experience the love of God, and accept Jesus as his Savior.

"You tell me, Doctor, to think of my other four children. Well, indeed I am thinking of my other children. They'll welcome their new brother as a gift from God, not visit him in an institution! They'll learn what it truly means to be a servant of the Lord. They'll come to understand that just because John looks differently than they do, doesn't mean he's any less deserving of God's love, and certainly not any less deserving of a Christian family. My husband and I made a promise to each other before the Lord Jesus that we would accept any, and all, children that He would bless us with. John is indeed a blessing."

Dr. Phillips immediately, repeated his counsel. "Irene, John will need very skilled care, very specialized care. Once again, I advise you, this care will be very time-consuming and very challenging, even for a skilled specialist. These responsibilities will be extremely taxing on you, both physically and emotionally. It's an impossible demand that you're placing upon yourself. How will you ever manage? Besides, you'll be able to visit John as frequently as you desire."

Richard and Laura remained absolutely silent. They both knew Irene well enough to understand that this was her chosen battle. It was best not to interrupt, at least not at this point. To engage themselves in the conversation at this point may result in someone becoming a casualty of this war of words!

"How will I manage, Doctor? I honestly don't know how I'll manage," responded a still sobbing Irene clutching onto her tissues. "I guess I have no answers to your questions, just as you have no answers for my questions. I do know this much: my Lord promises, 'The Lord is the One who goes before you; He will be with you. He will not fail you or forsake you. Do not fear or be dismayed' (Deuteronomy 31:8)."

Dr. Phillips softly interjected, "Irene, you're not being reasonable. This is an impossible task you are attempting to impose upon yourself."

Richard remained quiet, yet keenly attentive to the dialogue, as he kept nervously shifting in his chair. *Doctor, you have no idea how futile your efforts will be to take John away from Irene. I fought easier battles in Germany and Italy during World War II!* Richard knew he would inevitably stand with Irene. It was not the journey he ever thought he would embark upon with his wife, after all, who could have imagined such circumstances? Just as Richard had committed himself to the war effort, risking his own life for his country, all the more would he decisively fight this battle with his comrade for life, Irene.

"Dr. Phillips, when you started this conversation, you encouraged us to take this one step at a time. I suppose that's the best answer I can give you regarding how I'll manage the demands of appropriately caring for John. I'll take this one day at a time. Isn't that precisely what the Lord's Prayer teaches us to do? 'Give us this day, our daily bread' (Matthew 6:11). It doesn't teach us to pray for a week's supply of bread, or a month's portion of bread, or a year's supply of bread. It teaches us to rely on the Lord for our sustenance on a daily basis.

"Wasn't this the same lesson learned by the Israelites in their sojourn through the desert? God provided them strictly with a day's supply of manna. Those who attempted to hoard more than a day's supply awoke only to find the excess manna spoiled with worms (Exodus 16:4,20)!

"That is precisely what I shall do. I'll take this one step at a time, believing the Lord walks before me, and I shall carefully follow in His footsteps. I'll take this one day at a time, praying, 'Give us this day, our daily bread.' God most certainly did not bestow this gift of John upon us, for us to abandon this precious gift to an institution. Likewise, my Lord surely will not abandon me! I believe that from the depths of my heart."

"Oh, Irene," sighed Dr. Phillips, "consider the years yet to come. The baby you held earlier will not be the same child in years to come. John's condition will worsen exponentially with time. The demands will only increase beyond measure, beyond the capacity of what one mere mortal would be able to accomplish."

"Trust me, Doctor, I never fathomed this would happen to a simple, country girl from Ovid, New York. All I ever naively dreamed of was raising a large family of healthy children. I know the Bible promises, 'Don't worry about tomorrow, for tomorrow will bring its own worries. Today's trouble is enough for today' (Matthew 6:34). Am I honestly perplexed and afraid? There is no scale created by man that can measure the heaviness I now feel in my heart. None! Do I honestly feel anxious embarking on this incredible journey? You better believe I do! Yet again, the Bible says,

'Cast all your anxieties on Him because He cares for you' (I Peter 5:7).

Dr. Phillips, you know I possess the utmost respect for you, but this is a done deal. This is the biggest leap of faith I've ever made in my life."

Dr. Phillips was speechless. He politely excused himself, explaining that he had other patients to see, he promised to return later.

Laura stood up and volunteered to go over to the house to assure that everything was clean and ready for Irene and John's arrival home. "You made me very proud to be your mother today, Darling. I'll do all I can to be of assistance." Laura kissed her daughter and subsequently gave Richard a long embrace. Richard couldn't thank his mother-in-law sufficiently for the support of her presence.

The day finally arrived for John to come home. Irene could not help but feel nervous now that she was flying solo in caring for John and the other four children. Without a doubt, the most painful experience for Irene was denying her strong maternal instincts to hug John. It felt as though someone was suffocating her. Each time she heard her new baby cry, she felt as though someone was kicking her in the stomach as, time and time again, she found it torturous to deny her maternal instincts.

As Irene lay John carefully in his bassinet, she gently restrained both his hands to the sides with sterile gauze as the doctor advised. His outstretched arms inevitably reminded Irene of Jesus on the cross. As John, with his bright blue, innocent eyes, looked directly at his mother's face, Irene fell to her knees sobbing, "Give us this day, our daily bread!"

Irene had her first experience changing John's dressings. She gently removed the external padding. As Irene began slowly and gingerly to remove the gauze, John writhed and cried. Irene cried right along with him. If only her tears could heal his wounds, there most certainly were sufficient tears to heal his entire body. Next, she gently washed and rinsed his body with the medicated soap, paying particular attention to his hands, feet, and underarms, whose skin was already fusing. Indeed, his back did look as though he sustained third-degree burns. Finally, Irene began the arduous task of carefully placing fresh strips of sterile gauze, covered in vaseline, across John's body. As John once again writhed with pain, Irene felt as though her heart had been placed through a meat grinder. Alas! This was only day one!

That night, Irene limped to her bed, mentally, emotionally, and physically exhausted. *Tomorrow is a new day.* She prayed more fervently than she had ever prayed in her entire life, "Give us this day, our daily bread," and quickly fell into a deep sleep.

When John was approximately three months old, Irene discovered she was pregnant with their sixth child. Naturally, her first question addressed to the doctor related to the potential of another baby being born with DEB. Her mind was clouded with deep concern. The doctor gave his best assurance that the chances of this repeating itself were extremely remote due to the rarity of the recessive gene. The doctor actually insisted that Irene dismiss this concern from her mind immediately. Those words from the doctor were like rays of sunshine dispersing the clouds of concern from her mind.

Irene shared the exciting news with Richard. She quickly relayed the assurance of the doctor that the baby would not likely be born with DEB. As was the case with Irene, Richard received this news with great relief. While no one had ever heard even a whisper of complaint from Richard or Irene regarding their plight in life, nonetheless, neither parent could comprehend the demands of having two children with DEB. They just felt their shoulders were not strong enough to carry such a cross. Irene thought of the old adage that her mother so often repeated, "The Lord never places a cross on our shoulder too heavy for us to carry." Irene found immeasurable solace in those words. When they prayed together that night, Richard and Irene thanked the Lord for their newest child, now on its way to becoming a member of the O'Brien Clan.

The due date for the arrival of the baby was, ironically, in early July. As a very pregnant Irene prepared for the joyous celebration of John's first birthday on July 1, 1954, she reflected upon the whirlwind of challenges and turmoil that one, single year had presented to her as unexpectedly as a funnel cloud descends suddenly from the sky. Yet, the Lord had been faithful, providing her with her daily sustenance.

Within a few days, Irene and Richard gave birth to their sixth child. As the doctor had assured them, their newest son was born healthy with absolutely no symptoms of DEB. Irene and Richard paid a visit to the hospital chapel together to pray and thank the Lord for a healthy son.

On one occasion when the newborn baby was brought to the room, Irene held the baby and announced to Richard, "We're naming this child Stephen James. He looks just like a Stephen James, doesn't he, Richard?" Irene inquired.

Dick immediately nodded his head in complete agreement, adding, "He most certainly does," all the while wondering silently to himself what a "Stephen" was supposed to look like. Richard just simply concluded that these matters were among the multitude of mysteries relegated solely to women and were no part of being a man!

Stephen James soon joined his five siblings at home. Irene found the array of tasks involved in caring for five children, including an infant, along with providing the time consuming, skilled care for John, to be quite daunting, to say the least. She was strengthened by her faith, implored the Lord to sustain her with His "daily bread," and remembered that the Lord loved a "cheerful giver," as she daily laid down her own life for her children's sake. Irene was radiant with joy!

Chapter Four

GREATER LOVE HATH NO MAN

Not long after Stephen's birth, employment opportunity brought Richard, and the remainder of the ever-expanding O'Brien Clan, to the suburbs of Buffalo, New York. Their new abode was approximately a two and a half hour drive from Ovid and a three hour drive from Ithaca. It was not in reality that great of a distance, but it may as well have been a trans-Atlantic move as far as Irene was concerned. She never felt so distant and separated from her mother, Laura, in her entire lifetime. Irene terribly missed the proximity of her mother, and the support and assistance her mother's presence afforded to her daunting responsibilities. Irene missed even the sound of her mother's voice after becoming so accustomed to speaking with her on a daily basis. Laura always possessed the precise words Irene needed to hear. Long-distant phone calls were not cheap in those days, and besides, telephone conversations were no substitute for the presence of her mother.

What was even more taxing on Irene's mind was the awareness that she needed to find a new pediatrician that she could trust implicitly with John's care. Life had taught Irene that many doctors were completely unfamiliar with John's condition. Finding the right doctor was a top priority for Richard and Irene in this new venture of their life. Irene prayed fervently, and finally found a doctor that she absolutely loved and in whom she deeply trusted. She couldn't thank the Lord enough!

Just as the doctor in Ithaca had advised, John's condition was worsening, it seemed, almost by the day. Irene felt so disheartened every time she discovered new blisters, new scabs, and new scars. This translated into increased suffering for John and heartache for Irene. John's hands had become completely fused, resulting in "clubbed hands." The same was true with his feet. Slowly, John was becoming progressively crippled. Irene's proficiency in the skill of caring for John seemed to be in a race with the progression and complications of the disease.

John had frequent episodes of the inflammation of the eyelids as the doctor had previously explained. Yes, there were many occasions when both eyes were inflamed simultaneously, causing him to be blind, as bandages covered his eyes. This required that John be hand-fed. All John's meals required special preparation due to the increasing blistering within his mouth and the subsequent loss of some of his teeth.

Irene and Richard worked in tandem to assure that the needs of the other children were not ignored. Naturally, Richard needed his employment to sustain his family. However, whenever he was home, he contributed as best he was able in assisting his wife.

Richard and Irene both recognized that there would be additional sacrifices they would need to make in caring for John. For example, they were unable to indulge themselves, even with a brief get away together, as couples so often do, to find respite from the demands of family life and just spend some serene time with each other. There was just no one available to provide proper care for John. Additionally, the family would be denied the typical summer vacation travels enjoyed by many other families because it would be too taxing on John. Such vacations would have to be restricted to visiting grandparents in Ithaca and Ovid.

Irene took heart in the Scripture, "Greater love than this has no man, than to lay down his life for his friends" (John 15:13). Irene would gladly lay down her life for John, and her other children, because she loved each of them beyond measure. In Irene's mind, any sacrifice was far outweighed by the blessing of the gift of John. The taxing demands and sacrifices placed upon Irene's life were no match for the blessing John was to the O'Brien family. She never regretted bringing John home to the loving environment of a deeply, Christian family instead of placing him in an institution; not even for a second.

As some of the children were of school age, Irene embraced the opportunity for doing the laundry, preparing the meals, doing the dishes, making the beds, polishing the furniture, sterilizing baby bottles, and various other household chores. The demands of John's care constantly interrupted Irene's work, yet somehow she managed to get everything accomplished. She could not do the grocery shopping until Richard returned home from work with the car. He then would be able to watch over John and the other children while Irene shopped.

Irene and Richard were blessed to meet many new and wonderful friends through their church and in their neighborhood. These friends, as time would tell, were to become life-long friends that would prove their love and loyalty to Richard and Irene, time and time again. If the passage of time and the measure of support, extended during extreme trials, were the litmus tests of true friendships, these friends passed summa cum laude. Both Richard and Irene were most grateful to God, not for just one faithful friend, but for a multitude of strong, Christian friends.

Irene's circle of friends often wondered among themselves what they could do to be of assistance to her. They often spoke of how they never once heard her complain. All those who ever met Irene, friends and strangers alike, remarked what a joyous woman she was and how much they loved to be in her company. "Why, you wouldn't think she had a problem in the world!" they all concluded. It was a testament to Irene's faith and her personal relationship with the Lord.

When Irene and Richard promised to accept any and all children that the Lord would send them, they were very sincere. Later that year, Irene discovered she was pregnant with her seventh child. The doctor once again admonished Irene to dismiss any concerns that this baby would be born with DEB, citing that it was just too rare of a disease.

"Put those concerns out of your mind immediately and be excited. Go home and share the good news with your family!" advised the doctor.

The ride home from the doctor's office in a friend's car was an experience filled with excitement and laughter. Irene wondered out loud if she would be the mother of a dozen children.

The friend added, "Why don't you make it a baker's dozen?"

"Oh sure, after you!" Irene quickly retorted.

Excitement filled the wells of Irene's soul to the very brim. This is precisely what she had always wanted, a large family. With several children enrolled in school, this seemed to be the perfect time for welcoming an addition to the ever-expanding O'Brien family. Irene was further excited that the due date for the unborn was near Valentine's Day. She thought how wonderful it would be to have a Valentine's baby!

It was an extremely close call, but the baby arrived the day after Valentine's Day, February 15, 1957. Irene thought of her mother's old adage, "A baby will come when it's good and ready to come."

While his wife was in labor, Richard had purchased an assortment of blue and pink candy cigars, not yet knowing the gender of the baby. He was nervously pacing the corridor and whispering prayers in the chapel. *You would think this would be something I'm used to by now.* Yet, Richard kept pacing those corridors as if he was going to wear a hole in the soles of his shoes. He diligently kept watch for a nurse to come and bring him the good news. Because the baby was born so close to Valentine's Day, Richard had decided to buy his wife a gift. He found what he thought was the perfect, ideal gift: a gold necklace with a single, red rose hanging from the chain.

Finally, a nurse came out of nowhere and startled Richard as she loudly called, "Mr. Richard O'Brien." Richard rushed toward the nurse and introduced himself. The nurse, very politely and professionally, requested that Richard follow her to the appropriate room.

Richard jovially inquired, "Well, do you want a blue or pink cigar?"

The nurse turned to him with a very stoic face, and replied, "I guess that will be a pink cigar. You have a new daughter, Mr. O'Brien." Richard broke out with such a broad smile that it hurt his cheeks.

As he entered the room, grinning from ear to ear, he suddenly, and unexpectedly, felt as though he had run into a brick wall. The somber emotion in that room immediately erased the smile from his face. He felt his heart drop to the pit of his stomach.

Initially at a loss for words, he broke the icy silence with his sharply toned inquiry, "What seems to be the problem here?"

Richard's question caused Irene to break down with heart-wrenching sobs flowing with tears that could fill a bathtub. The doctor invited Richard to sit down on the chair.

"I didn't ask for a seat, Doctor. I asked, 'What seems to be the problem?' " Richard wasted no time rushing with haste to his wife's bedside.

The doctor reluctantly replied, "I'm so sorry to share this news with you, Richard. Your baby daughter was born with DEB."

Irene sobbed all the harder, until she felt the well of tears within her body had emptied itself, soaking her pillow. Richard held her hand tenderly. "Doctor, I thought you assured us that the possibility of this recurring was too remote to even worry about," Richard added with a firm voice.

The doctor then attempted to explain, "Since you now have a daughter with DEB, this suggests that both of you are carriers of this rare, recessive gene."

Richard and Irene could not hear the doctor's words. Their pain seemed to have made them deaf to the sound of his voice. They were not, at the moment, the least concerned with the medical jargon. Their only concern was for each other. They held hands and studied each other's eyes. If the eyes are truly the window to someone's soul, they each had empathy for the raging storm welling up in the other's soul. It was a storm that could sink the Titanic! Both husband and wife knew precisely the thoughts of the other, without the need to utter a single word. *Why, Lord? How are we ever going to carry this heavy cross, Lord? How will we ever be able to provide the requisite care for two children with DEB, along with providing for the other five children?*

Richard decided this was the appropriate time to present Irene with the gift he had purchased. He reached into his pocket and handed Irene a small box wrapped in blue paper with a pink bow.

"What's this for?" inquired Irene.

"It's for our almost-Valentine baby, Maureen Clare, and her wonderful mother."

"Wait a minute, Richard. Did I just hear you give a name to our new baby?" asked an astonished Irene.

"You most certainly did! Do you think only women can come up with names for children?" quipped Richard.

"I guess not. And I'm in love with that name!" responded Irene. "Where did you come up with it, Richard?"

"It came from somewhere very deep in my heart. Now, please open your gift!" he requested.

Irene wondered what was in that small box. She gently removed the pink bow and unwrapped the blue paper. It was a small, black box from a jewelry store. Irene couldn't resist another second in opening the mysterious box. Inside was the gold necklace with a single, red rose with two emerald leaves.

"Why, it's absolutely stunning! I love it! Thank you, Richard," exclaimed Irene.

Richard removed the necklace from the box and placed it around his wife's neck. "It's a beautiful flower, but a flower with thorns. When I look at the rose, my eyes go directly to the beautiful flower, our dear Maureen Clare. I don't even notice the thorns. Someone once said, 'Life is not about avoiding the storms. Life is about learning to dance in the rain.' I learned from you, Irene, as you told the doctors in Ithaca that John was a gift from the Lord.

"The same is true for Maureen. The Lord is truly calling us to lay down our lives. There will be trials and tribulations, I understand and accept that fact. I'll remain by your side as I vowed years ago, 'For better or for worse.' The Lord will sustain us with His daily provisions. We shall accept Maureen Clare as a gift from God. As we lay down our lives with the sacrifices entailed with her complex care, we shall concentrate on the beautiful flower that is Maureen, not on the thorns."

So, it came to pass, that Maureen Clare O'Brien was embraced as a special gift from God, albeit Richard and Irene were cognizant of the rough road and steep hill they were being asked to travel.

As the years passed, and nothing can make the years pass more quickly than raising seven children, the demands of caring for John and Maureen seemed insurmountable at times. Each year presented new challenges as they became more crippled and deformed. Irene was not getting any younger and the stress certainly was taking a toll on her. Some close, Christian friends of Irene had agreed, with the very best of intentions, to provide Irene with some respite.

They promised Irene they would do John and Maureen's dressings one day each week. The first volunteer literally passed out on the bedroom floor when she saw, for the first time, John and Maureen's naked bodies and smelled the soiled bandages. This friend was accustomed to seeing them only in specially designed gowns that a talented seamstress would supply for John and Maureen. Nothing could have prepared this friend for what had become a matter of routine for Irene.

"I just could never do what the Lord has asked of you, Irene," confessed the friend.

The next volunteer was to assist on Fridays during the season of Lent. As it was in the first case, the second friend landed on the floor with a loud thud. When they awakened, they apologized profusely that they were too weak to keep their Lenten resolution. Irene comforted her friend by assuring her there was no need to apologize.

The friend could not restrain herself from exclaiming, "You know, Irene O'Brien, when you are out and about, you are consistently so joyous, so glamorous, and so mindful of other's needs. You present yourself as though you don't have a problem in the world. Today, I have come to realize that absolutely no one fully comprehends all that you are being asked to endure!"

Irene was noticing, with intricate detail, the progression of this debilitating disease. John and Maureen were to the point that their dressings needed to be adjusted during the day and certainly refreshed before retiring for the night. As they grew older, chronologically, their deformed bodies and stunted growth were increasingly noticeable. While they once could stand, and sometimes even walk, they were now confined to their kitchen chairs. Both John and Maureen needed to be carried to the bathroom, where passing a bowel movement was a long, laborious, and painful process. There was more extensive bleeding, especially on their backs, as the excessive blistering and scarring only became more prominent. It was inevitably time for John and Maureen to commence the regimen of monthly hospitalizations for blood transfusions.

The first experience in the hospital was a disaster. Irene entered the hospital room on the first day; John and Maureen's dressings had been completed by the nursing staff and the transfusions were already in place. John and Maureen looked extremely uncomfortable. Irene was abhorred as she examined the dressings only to discover that the bandages were incorrectly layered and lacked sufficient Vaseline. The bandages were slipping off, causing friction on their frail skin, which undoubtedly would create new blisters. She then observed that one of the transfusions was infiltrating and causing excessive bruising instead of properly entering the bloodstream. Finally, she noticed that the tubing was firmly secured to John and Maureen's arms with adhesive tape on portions where there was good skin.

Irene immediately called for a doctor. She first pointed out the infiltrating transfusion. The doctor apologized profusely and explained how difficult it was to find a vein that could sustain the needle. He then gently removed the transfusion and searched for a viable vein. Success came only after the doctor inserted the needle into a vein in John's forehead.

Next, Irene brought the doctor's attention to the slipping bandages due to their incorrect placement. She explained how this unnecessary friction would cause more extensive blistering. Once again, the doctor apologized and offered to call a nurse to correct the situation. John and Maureen implored their mother to be the one to do it, not a nurse. Irene therefore politely refused the doctor's offer, stating she would correct the bandages herself.

Finally, Irene asked the doctor why adhesive tape was used and placed so tightly on their skin. She once again explained how removing the tape would most definitely be painful and cause blistering on the skin. The doctor and Irene worked in unison trying to remove the tape as John and Maureen cried in pain. The doctor assured Irene they would utilize a different form of tape in the future, but the present circumstances had inflicted terrible wounds on John and Maureen that would take months to heal, if they ever healed at all.

From that day forward, and in the years to come, Irene would set her alarm to 3:00 a.m. whenever John and Maureen were hospitalized. She would arrive by 4:00 a.m. and complete the dressings before the doctors were ready for the transfusions. She would help find a suitable vein on their "butterfly wing" skin. Irene had indeed laid down her life for her children; it could not be said that she lived even one day for herself.

As the years passed, and John and Maureen were frequent guests of the hospital, they began forging deep relationships with the doctors and nurses. Soon, it seemed as though everyone in the hospital came to know and love John and Maureen; they also deeply respected their mother, Irene, who was by now, singing the praises of the hospital for the excellent care they provided her children.

The Bishop of Buffalo, the Most Reverend James McNulty, resided down the street from the hospital. The

Bishop came to learn of John and Maureen. When they were hospitalized, the Bishop would walk down the street to pay them a visit. John and Maureen were delighted! If Irene happened be in the room at the time of one of his visits, she would always genuflect to kiss the Bishop's ring, as was the tradition at the time. The Bishop was unsuccessful in his attempts to persuade Irene that her actions were not necessary. Irene's problem was that she required the Bishop's assistance to help her to her feet. On one occasion, she almost pulled the Bishop down on top of her! This scene caused John and Maureen to howl with laughter. Irene loved to witness them laugh; it was a miracle as far as she was concerned.

One night, while a friend was visiting John and Maureen during evening visiting hours, John requested that the friend secure a wheelchair and take him for a walk. The friend readily agreed and promised to do the same for Maureen when he returned with the chair. As the friend was wheeling John to places in the hospital that John had never before seen, they passed a patient's room with the door closed. No sooner had they passed this room than John insisted he wanted to be turned around and taken back to that room with the closed door. The family friend advised John that the door was probably closed for a purpose: perhaps there were friends visiting, or a doctor was performing a procedure on the patient, or the doctor was having a private conversation with the parent.

"A closed door is a request for privacy," the friend explained.

John was insistent that they return to the room and would accept no excuses. He explained to his friend, that as they passed the room, the Lord had given him a message for the people in the room. He expressed to the friend that the message was simply, "The Lord has heard your prayers. Your child will be fine tomorrow." Well, the friend certainly did not want an argument with the Lord, and obediently turned around and knocked on the closed door for John.

A woman quietly opened the door, looked down at John and whispered, "Hello. May I help you with something?"

John peered into the room. He noticed a child asleep in the bed and a man, whom he presumed to be the father, standing at the end of the bed. Finally, John spoke up with great conviction in the tone of his voice.

"As I passed this room a moment ago, the Lord told me to go back and tell the people in the room that their child was going to be just fine tomorrow."

At this point, the mother and the father both began to cry. The mother explained to John that her son was going to have serious heart surgery in the morning. She added that she and her husband had just completed a prayer on behalf of their son, humbly asking the Lord for a sign that things would go fine. The mother expressed that no sooner had they finished their prayer than they heard a knock on the door.

"You'll never know how much this means to us," wept the mother.

The father came over to the door to introduce himself to John. "Hello, John, I'm the Mayor of Buffalo. I want you to take this number and call me if there's ever anything I can do for you. If you ever want to attend a basketball game or any other event at the auditorium, I'll guarantee you my parking place under the auditorium, as well as good seats for you and a guest."

Irene's discernment years ago continued to be proven correct; in bringing John and Maureen home to a Christian family, they would come to experience the love and power of God. These invalid children who were typically confined to their chairs at the kitchen table, had met, impacted, and become friends with the Bishop and Mayor of Buffalo. John and Maureen would win the hearts and souls of countless, multitudes of people from various walks of life.

Stephen once said of his brother John, "John has the capacity to make friends out of strangers, and family out of friends."

This all came to pass in the context of a warm, loving family; not in the confines of a cold, sterile institution. Yes, it cost Irene and Richard dearly, it cost them their very lives; "but greater love hath no man."

Irene teaches John and Maureen the tenets of their faith in the context of family life.

Time continued to pass more quickly than a rabbit being chased by a dog. In the early autumn of 1961, Irene discovered she was pregnant with her eighth child. For this pregnancy, there was no doctor in New York State that could promise the newborn would be spared the suffering of DEB. Scientifically, there was a 25% chance the baby could have DEB. All Richard and Irene could do was patiently wait upon the Lord to discover what His will was for their eighth child. "Those who wait upon the Lord, Will gain new strength; They will mount up with wings like eagles, They will run and not get tired, They will walk and not become weary" (Isaiah 40: 31).

On Thursday, April 12, 1962, Irene was taken to the hospital in labor. Laura and Michael were supervising the rest of the family. Laura had the entire family on their knees praying for hours awaiting the outcome. The "outcome" did not refer to the gender of the newborn baby, but rather, whether or not the baby would be born with DEB.

Finally, at 11:40 p.m. on the twelfth of April, Richard called to proudly announce the birth of his newest son. The son was born healthy, with no symptoms of DEB. Richard and Irene had previously decided on the name "Timothy Patrick" if the newborn was a boy. However, when Irene held her child, and gazed into those bright blue eyes and strawberry blonde hair, she exclaimed to Dick, "Oh my goodness, Richard! If this isn't a Patrick Timothy O'Brien, I don't know who is!"

For all Richard and Irene had deeply sacrificed, for all they had given up in laying down their lives in love for John and Maureen, Patrick was a breath of fresh, spring air. The joy in receiving Patrick Timothy gave both parents the wings of eagles that caused them to soar, giving them a new perspective on life, and a genuine reason to rejoice in the Lord.

Chapter Five

THE JOY OF THE LORD IS MY STRENGTH

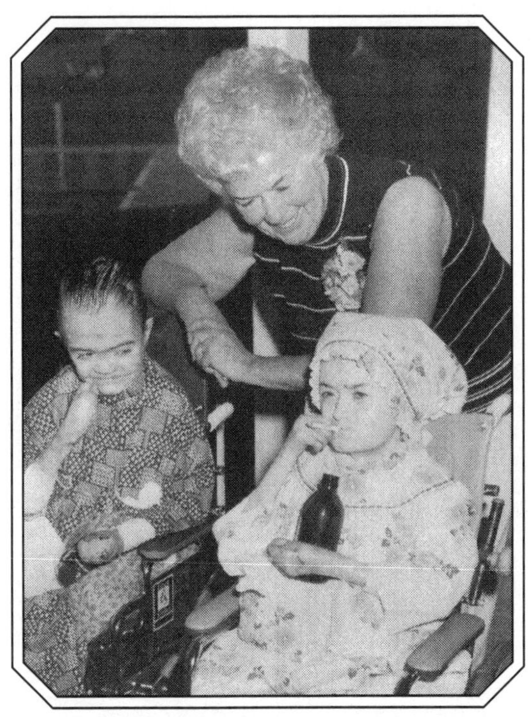

Maureen brings a smile to Irene's face by posing with a faux beer and cigarette!

The true miracle of the O'Brien family, was that despite the daily agony endured by John and Maureen, and all the extra demands of time involved in their appropriate care, the walls of their humble home constantly reverberated with hearty laughter. Nothing made Irene happier than to see John and Maureen laughing with their siblings. She was certain this miracle could only have happened in the context of a loving, Christian family, and not in an institution. The O'Brien siblings seemed unaffected by the DEB and treated John and Maureen as they treated each other, accepting the fact that John and Maureen were more restricted in their activities. John and Maureen were usually perched in two chairs around the kitchen table, the hub of excitement and activity in the O'Brien home.

As John and Maureen grew older, it became a custom to celebrate their birthdays in an extravagant fashion. Since they seldom could be taken outdoors due to their need to be in a temperature controlled environment, Irene would invite relatives, friends from the neighborhood, and her friends from prayer group and church over to the house. There were as many as fifty to seventy-five people in attendance for these joyous celebrations.

Being Irish Catholics, the parties usually began with a Mass celebrated in the house. John and Maureen touched and transformed the lives of all those privileged to meet them. Desperate for outside company, they spent months looking forward to celebrating their birthdays. They were extraordinary occasions that filled the house with laughter, and John and Maureen immensely enjoyed the company.

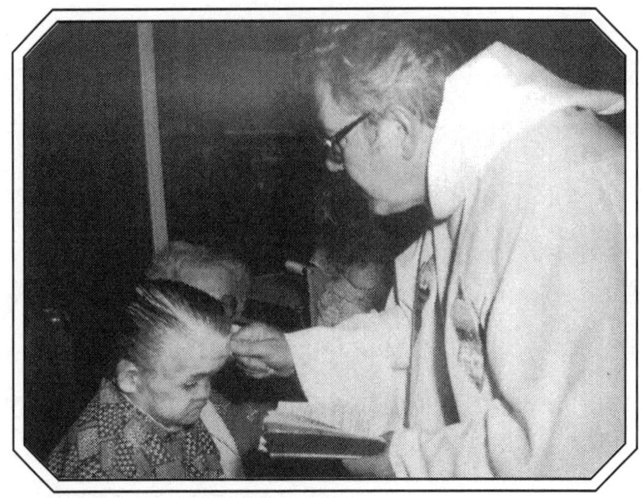

John and Maureen celebrate birthdays with a home Mass

Since it was so difficult to shop for something that John or Maureen could actually utilize, most of the guests presented them with cash gifts. John and Maureen appreciated this gesture. It empowered them and gave the two, who were so dependent on others to even feed them, a sense of their own independence. They could use their money to buy a gift for their mother, father, or siblings. If a friend stopped over to visit them around the kitchen table, they could offer to send out for a pizza. When the party was over, John and Maureen would count their cash donations and then carefully budget their income for another year. They seldom spent a nickel on themselves.

One year, John generously announced that his Christmas gift to the entire family would be to take everyone out to a nice restaurant for an exquisite, Christmas dinner. John felt this would spare his mother and father from all the laborious work of preparing a meal, setting a formal table, and then all the cleaning that follows a large holiday dinner at home. In this manner, everyone could spend the entire day at home, relaxing and enjoying each other's company.

The offer was enthusiastically received by an astonished family. They understood this would be good for John's ego and dared not decline his invitation. So, John began to carefully budget his money. This was his first attempt at such an adventure. He was not exactly sure of the cost involved. Yet John had been firm in his resolve to bring this to fruition. It would also be a special treat for he and Maureen since they rarely left the house. John felt like a man!

John dresses up to treat the family to a Christmas Dinner.

When the family was seated at the restaurant, John proudly sat at the head of the table. From this position of prestige, John proudly proclaimed, "Order anything you want! Dinner is on me." This was a new and thrilling experience for him, and the family was collectively making the most of the occasion. While John wasn't paying attention, Michael, prankster that he can be, slipped away and spoke to the waitress in private. Michael briefly explained the circumstances and instructed the waitress that when it came time to present the bill to John, she should tell John the total bill, including tax, would amount to $8,000. The waitress reluctantly agreed.

Everyone enjoyed their dinner immensely. The conversation was pleasant and filled with jovial laughter, and the food was exquisite. It truly was a Christmas that would never be forgotten. However, it was about to become better. The waitress complied with Michael's request and presented John with the bill, informing him that he owed $8,000 including the tax. John almost fell off his chair as a look of disbelief came over his face.

"What did you all eat that's costing $8,000?!" exclaimed John.

Stephen didn't miss a beat, correctly suspecting that Michael was behind all of this. "Well, I had Alaskan King Crab Legs. It must have cost them two or three thousand dollars just to get them in from Alaska," explained Stephen, with a serious face.

John retorted, "Well, who gave you permission to order Alaskan King Crab Legs?"

With a smirk on his face, Stephen replied, "John, you told us to order whatever we wanted."

"Well, I didn't tell you to order Alaskan King Crab Legs!" admonished John. "There's just no way I can afford to pay for this meal!" he lamented.

In unison, the entire table broke out in laughter and the waitress leaned over and whispered to John, "This is all a joke." You could see the blood flow back into John's cheeks as he experienced the relief that this had been a joke. Then, John joined the rest of the family with such boisterous laughter that the entire restaurant was looking at the O'Brien table. Irene leaned back in her chair, capturing the moment of John being fully embraced as a bonafide member of the family. The experience brought great joy to her soul. The words in the verse, "The joy of the Lord is your strength" (Nehemiah 8:10), crossed Irene's mind and heart.

Michael was not the only prankster living in the O'Brien house. Touch-tone telephones with long curled cords had become popular. Since they spent so much time alone at the kitchen table, as a gift, John and Maureen received a private line and a push-button phone with a speaker. It was an amazing feat of dexterity to watch John use a cotton swab pressed between his two clubbed hands to utilize the phone. Sometimes, he even used his mouth. Maureen had an easier time since she had use of some of her digits. The poignant question became whether or not this was a genuinely good idea in a household filled with pranksters.

Maureen must have been low on cash, or just plain bored and lonely, because when the kitchen was empty, she got on that telephone and called friend after friend. The messages to each friend were almost identical, "My mother is planning a party for us tomorrow at 6:00 p.m. She wondered if you could bring the mashed potatoes?" Maureen continued with the telephone calls until she had invited fifty people and covered the entire menu. John remained a silent co-conspirator!

On Saturday, Irene was at the beauty parlor having her hair done. Unexpectedly, a friend of the family was just leaving the same parlor. After greeting Irene and finishing a brief conversation, the friend gave Irene a hug good-bye and said, "I'll see you tomorrow at 6:00 p.m. I'm bringing the sliced ham."

Irene looked perplexed and inquired, "What's going on tomorrow night at 6:00 p.m.?"

"Well, the party at your house, of course," replied the friend.

With her eyebrows raised to the crown of her head, Irene exclaimed, "What party are you talking about?"

"Well, I received a phone call from Maureen, telling me that you're having fifty people over. Maureen relayed that you asked me to bring a sliced ham."

Irene's jaw hit the floor! It was probably a good thing for Maureen that Irene had a good half-hour left in the parlor! Irene wanted to rush home immediately, hair in curlers, to investigate the facts and start busily cleaning the house.

However, as she sat under the drier, a smile came across her face. She reached and felt the necklace with the single, red rose with the emerald leaves, that Dick had given her the day Maureen was born. Irene thanked the Lord for the gift of Maureen and how fully she was incorporated into the family. Irene's heart was bursting with joy. Maureen escaped with a mere stern warning that such antics should not be repeated or the phone would be disconnected.

John learned from his sister through that experience. The telephone resting on the kitchen table, with its speaker, could easily be used to manipulate circumstances to their advantage. John's day finally arrived. The rest of the O'Brien family had a standing reservation for 6:00 p.m. at a restaurant an hour's drive away from the house. Therefore, they would all have to leave the house by 5:00 p.m. One of John's favorite friends was scheduled to come to the house by 5:00 p.m. to visit with John and Maureen while the rest of the family went out for dinner. Make no mistake, John loved a busy kitchen. Yet he also appreciated some private conversation with friends. Once again, it gave John a sense of independence.

So, when the kitchen was empty, he took his cotton swab between his two clubbed hands and called the friend. John wanted additional private time with his friend. Therefore, he told the friend that the family changed the reservation to 5:00 p.m. and therefore, would need him at the house by 4:00 p.m. The friend assured John that would be no problem. This time, Maureen was John's co-conspirator.

John strategically waited until 3:00 p.m. and then told the other members of the family that the restaurant had called and explained that due to a large party at the restaurant, they had to move the O'Brien reservation up by one hour. This meant that everyone had to scurry to get freshened up and be out of the house within an hour. That mission was accomplished. En route to the restaurant, the other members of the family were busily remarking how unusual, and how rude, it was for the restaurant to call on such short notice to advance the reservation by a full hour.

The family arrived at the restaurant precisely at 5:00 p.m. Upon entering the restaurant, Michael informed the hostess it was the O'Brien party. The hostess looked down at her schedule and announced, "I'm sorry, Mr. O'Brien, I have you reserved for 6:00 p.m. and regretfully we have no empty tables at this time."

Everyone came to the same realization at precisely the same moment. This was one of John's antics! While everyone else was initially disturbed with John, Irene's eyes twinkled. "John is no different from the lot of you! That brings great joy to my heart. Don't you understand, he wanted an extra hour alone with his friend."

On the ride home from the restaurant, Irene's heart was filled with joy, and those moments of joy were as refreshing as a cool, northerly breeze on a hot, humid July day. She was so ecstatic that her family was a genuine, single, cohesive unit. There were no distinctions among those afflicted with DEB and those who were not, at least not in the way her children related to each other. Nothing made Irene happier!

Irene's favorite story was one shared by Stephen. Stephen had taken John to a basketball game at the auditorium in Buffalo. After leaving the game, Stephen carried John to the vehicle, placing him in the back seat. Upon departing the auditorium, Stephen was pulled over by the police for a brake light that was not functioning. The police officer came to the window to request a driver's license and car registration. The officer also looked at John in the rear seat using his flashlight.

John did not want this event to spoil an otherwise perfect evening enjoyed with his brother. John had his solution. From the back seat, within hearing distance of the officer, John kept repeating, "Stephen! Tell him I'm handicapped! Tell him I'm handicapped!"

Irene just laughed upon hearing the story. She marveled how John's self-image did not primarily include being handicapped. Apparently, as far as John was concerned, his condition was not noticeable to the officer upon his first glance at him. Rather, it was something that the officer needed to be told!

"This is the miracle of John being fully embraced as a member of a family who loves him and treats him no differently than the other members of the family. Honestly, it brings me such joy!" Irene proclaimed to the rest of the family. "You'll never appreciate how such incidents strengthen my soul."

The expression of joy that moved the hearts of multitudes!

Chapter Six

IN MY WEAKNESS, HIS POWER IS MADE PERFECT

Years continued to pass as if someone had placed the family clock on speed dial. However, today was a special occasion that generated much excitement. This was the day the O'Brien family was moving into a newly constructed home in a budding new neighborhood, not far from their previous home. The realtor disclosed that the empty, new house had been struck by lightning, but all the necessary repairs had been completed. No one thought much about the fact that the house had been hit by lightning. After all, lightning never strikes the same place twice, or does it?

This house had more square footage than the previous home. More importantly, the home had two and a half baths, a modern necessity for sprouting teens! The boys were assigned to sleep in the master bedroom with bunk beds and their own private bath. The girls had their private bath at the top of the stairs, and they were delighted. The older siblings were already in their teens; John was eleven, Maureen was seven, and Patrick Timothy was only three.

This house would become the final stop of the O'Brien family. It would eventually become the empty nest for Dick and Irene, as the O'Brien fledglings would soar to begin their own lives.

John and Maureen received a new view in the kitchen, but they occupied the same chairs, with their backs facing the kitchen wall. This is where they spent most of their day, watching a portable television, one of their most recent gifts. It was also from these chairs that John and Maureen watched their siblings grow older, acquiring licenses to drive, and spending more and more time out of the house. John and Maureen missed their siblings during the evenings, but they thoroughly enjoyed meeting the dates they brought home on occasion.

John had his own method of testing the true character of a stranger; he would extend his right, clubbed hand, bandaged with greasy vaseline, to greet someone with a handshake. If the person retreated, winced, or ignored his polite gesture, it did not matter how well-spoken the person was; you were off John's list permanently. However, if one returned John's gesture and took his hand to shake it, you passed John's litmus test as a worthy character.

As the other siblings grew still older, John and Maureen's deformity and stunted growth became more apparent to both of them. It was difficult for them to watch their siblings beginning to acquire a sense of independence, while the road they were traveling was only leading them to become more dependent on others. At times, John and Maureen envied the lives of their older siblings. Who could ever forget Maureen's question to her mother, as she watched from her kitchen chair, as her older sisters were getting formally dressed for the prom? Her sisters looked so beautiful to Maureen.

"Mom, will I ever be able to get dressed up so beautifully and go out on a date to a prom?"

How does a mother answer such an unexpected, heart-wrenching question? Irene once again felt a dagger pierce her heart. She wanted a miracle so badly for John and Maureen. She had prayed daily since the day they were born, that they would receive a miracle. There were times when Irene would privately prostrate herself on the floor in deep intercession for a miracle. She knew all of her church and prayer group friends joined in her intentions.

John and Maureen looked to be the same chronological age due to the deformity of the disease. In fact, there were many occasions when people mistook them as twins. Nothing could possibly irritate John and Maureen more than to be mistaken as twins! Be assured, John and Maureen could not have been more different in terms of their personalities. John was a wild tiger with a boisterous personality and Maureen was a porcelain doll, a precious, fragile, gentle doll. Maureen was much more sensitive, frail, and prone to tears. John had a stronger and sometimes stubborn attitude.

As different as they were in terms of their personalities, they nonetheless shared a deep, inseparable bond with each other. They shared the same kitchen by day and the same bedroom by night. More poignantly, they shared the same, rare disease. They listened to each other's agony as their dressings were being changed by an aging Irene. John and Maureen intrinsically knew that there was no other person who could genuinely understand the complexity of their bond. John and Maureen were their own support group. They understood that others may be witnesses of their suffering, but those very same people never experienced the suffering as they experienced it. Others did not need to fall asleep wondering why this disease was inflicted upon them and not their other siblings. No other person obsessed over questions of what further suffering awaited them in the future. So, although at times they became engaged in a war of words, they possessed an unbreakable bond of love.

Richard III, or Ricky as he was known to his siblings and friends, was a champion athlete. Ricky earned trophies in any sport he played. During his high school years, wrestling was Ricky's major sport. John and Maureen admired Rick for his strength and agility. They especially enjoyed watching him prepare for a wrestling match. To meet his weigh-in requirements, Ricky layered himself in a multitude of gray sweatsuits; the final layer consisted of some plastic rain gear. He would then proceed to run up the stairs from the basement, all the way to the top of the second story and then back down again. This process would last a half-hour and it was sheer entertainment for John and Maureen. They laughed every time they heard Ricky grunting with exhaustion and yelled out loud to boost his adrenaline.

When Rick won trophy after trophy, no one was more proud of him than his brother John. John wished so badly that he could be a championship athlete just like his brother. John was keenly aware of just how immensely proud his father was of Ricky each time he brought home a trophy. John noticed that his father never missed one of his wrestling matches and even attended many of his practices. John realized that Ricky was his father's namesake, but nonetheless, he wished he could likewise make his father so proud. Unlike Maureen, who tearfully inquired of her mother if she would ever attend a prom, John felt no compunction to ask his mother if he would ever be a champion athlete. John feared the answer to such a question.

Well, Irene came to discover that lightning can indeed strike the same place twice. When the older children were teenagers, Irene learned that her mother was terminally ill with lung cancer. She moved Laura into the house immediately, to care for her and pray for a miracle. She made every flavored milkshake imaginable so that her mother would gain strength. Irene bathed her, curled her hair, and administered all her medications. She was extremely devoted to her mother and prayed for that miracle incessantly, requesting the family to join her and pray with her in faith for a miracle. Eventually, Laura had to be placed in a local hospital.

All of Irene's friends felt deep empathy for her, understanding the immeasurable love she had for her mother. They considered Irene to be a strong woman, after all, she readily assumed the care of her mother while still needing to attend to the ever increasing demands of John and Maureen.

It was a Sunday morning when the phone call came from the hospital. Richard answered the phone as Michael Corcoran nervously paced the floor. The hospital informed Dick that Laura had taken a turn for the worse. Dick drove his father-in-law to the hospital. As they arrived at the hospital, they were greeted and subsequently informed that Mrs. Corcoran had passed peacefully.

Irene mourned the loss of her mother who was taken to Ovid and buried in Holy Cross Cemetery. There, down the third road of the cemetery, almost to the end of the drive, on the left-hand side, Laura Mae was put to rest. Irene felt a void in her heart that she knew would never be filled. She thought about her Lord and how He initially cried at the news of his friend Lazarus dying. This assured Irene that the Lord understood her emotions.

Just a few years later, Irene also took her father into her home to provide for his care. She had a contractor build a remodeled basement into an apartment with its own kitchen. Irene expected her father to spend most of his day upstairs but wanted to provide him with his own private retreat. Irene took meticulous care of her dad, all the while continuing with the demands of John and Maureen. She had made a routine of thinking of others before she attended to herself. She was becoming a living example of the scripture, "Whoever wants to be first must be the least of all and servant of all" (Mark 9:35).

The living situation with Irene's father did not last for more than a couple of months. It is known that seniors can have a hard time adjusting to new living situations. So, Michael Corcoran moved back to Geneva, New York and ironically, ended up occupying the same apartment he had vacated months earlier. Michael's departure had nothing to do with his love for Irene or his grandchildren. He just felt at home in Geneva and he could walk to every destination he needed to visit; the grocery store, the drug store, the cleaners, the barber shop, and most importantly the church, were all in walking distance. Michael required his independence and all the O'Briens fully understood.

In a matter of a few short years, a phone call came very early one morning. Irene realized that no good news ever came at that hour. She blessed herself before answering the phone. Her brother Glenn was on the other end of the line. He informed Irene that their father had passed away in the middle of the night. Michael Corcoran had even walked himself to the hospital.

The mail came later that same afternoon. In the mail, was a letter from Michael to his daughter Irene. In the letter,

Michael expressed his affection for her. He concluded the letter with these words, "Just came from the doctor's today; he says I'm as strong as a horse. But the good Lord knows I'm ready to go today."

Michael Corcoran was buried in Holy Cross Cemetery, down the third driveway almost to the end of the road. There, on the left hand side of the drive, next to his wife, Michael Corcoran was laid to rest. Irene stood in the cemetery, feeling like a boxer knocked unconscious on the mat of life. Irene thought of the inscription on the watch she had presented to her father on the occasion of her wedding. *Dad, a day hasn't gone by that those words weren't true.*

Christmas came all too early that year. Ricky and Michael were attending the same college. Ricky was still the stellar athlete and wrestler that he was in high school. Stephen was in high school and Patrick was still in grade school. Sharon Ann had gotten married, and Cassie was professionally employed. Irene knew that she would miss her father terribly this holiday season, as was the case when her mother passed.

Irene was resolved in assuring that the family celebrated the holidays in the typical O'Brien fashion. This included a lavish dinner on Christmas Eve, followed by drinks and conversation, surrounded by the wood burning fireplace, the family Christmas tree, and countless candles adorning the mantle. It created an ambiance that relaxed everyone and almost made them wish it could last forever. Gifts were not opened until Christmas morning after John and Maureen's dressings were completed. There was a large Christmas breakfast served in the kitchen, while the dining room table was always reserved for the formal dinner on Christmas night.

After completing the Christmas dinner meal and cleaning up, the O'Briens customarily settled back into the living room. Logs were aglow in the fireplace, as soft holiday music could be heard on the brand new sound system. Candles were again lit on the fireplace and there was, once again, that magical ambiance to enjoy. The O'Briens sat in the warmth and comfort of the living room and laughed hysterically, as they recalled the Christmases of years past when they were wee little children who still believed in Santa Claus.

All the siblings recalled how their mother, beginning after Halloween, would commence with her threats, "There will be no Christmas in the O'Brien house this year if that misbehavior doesn't stop!"

They remembered how their father secretly left the house and dressed up as Santa Claus as part of the Christmas Eve tradition. The problem was, Dick was so obnoxious in the roll that he always frightened the children to the extent that they were almost afraid of his impending return when they were fast asleep. The siblings recalled how they would wake up at 5:00 a.m. only to be sent back to bed by their parents for another hour. Huddled in the same bed, they would take turns counting to sixty as they counted down the minutes until they could rush downstairs. Everyone was thoroughly enjoying what seemed to be the most perfect Christmas ever!

The conversation and laughter, in front of the fireplace, was interrupted by a knock on the front door. Rick leaped from his seat announcing, "That's for me. A few of us are going snowmobiling. I won't be out late," Ricky added as he looked directly at his father.

Dick responded, "Well, if you have a problem, don't call us, we'll call you!"

Rick's friend laughed. Then Ricky did something that was very uncharacteristic of him. He picked up his wine glass. "I'd like to propose a toast," Rick announced to his family. "Here's to the best Christmas we've ever enjoyed and here's to the best family that ever lived. I love you all!" With that, he finished his wine and dashed out the front door with his friends. The sound of the snowmobiles could be heard departing the front lawn.

Everyone's consensus was that it had been another perfect Christmas. The O'Briens began to retire, exhausted from a long day filled with love and laughter. Dick was the last to retire after assuring the red, glowing, coals in the fireplace were extinguished. Everyone fell fast asleep, undoubtedly dreaming of the joyous Christmas they had just experienced.

Suddenly, the sound of the telephone ringing woke the entire household like the trumpet of an archangel raising the dead. There was a telephone extension in Dick and Irene's bedroom. Irene insisted that Dick be the one to answer the phone, as she was visibly frantic with a look of terror in her eyes reminiscent of a Hollywood horror flick.

"Calm down, Irene," Dick said to his wife. "It's probably just Rick with some flimsy excuse as to why he missed his curfew after promising me he wouldn't be late."

"Yes, this is Mr. O'Brien," Dick spoke into the phone. "Yes, Dr. Higgins, I have a son named Richard. What seems to be the problem?"

As Irene listened to Dick's half of the conversation, she began to panic, and kept whispering to Dick, "Who is it? What's the problem?"

Dick motioned to Irene to be still, so he could hear the voice on the other end of the line. However, there was no silencing Irene. Instantly she began running through the house checking that everyone was awake and imploring them to begin praying immediately. Irene's instincts told her that the house once again had been hit by lightning! She was not ready for the subsequent turmoil.

As Dick hung up the phone, Irene wailed so loudly that she could have easily awakened the neighbors. "What's the matter, Dick? What's happened to Ricky?" Irene's voice was trembling like that of a fearful, little child.

Richard explained to her, "Rick has been in a serious accident with the snowmobile. He's in a coma at the County Hospital, in critical condition. I need to get dressed and leave immediately." Cassie bravely accompanied her father to the hospital, while Dick instructed Michael to wait at home and look after his mother.

Irene screamed and fell to the floor lamenting, "Oh, my Lord, please, no! I can endure no more! I've been your faithful servant and I beg of you, Lord Jesus, please, nothing more!" As the car pulled out the driveway, Irene yelled to Dick, "Call as soon as you can!"

Each minute that passed without a telephone call seemed like an agonizing hour. The debate wavered whether it was good news or bad news that the phone call had not yet come. It was like wondering if a jury deliberating for a long or short time was a good or bad omen. The nervous energy in the house was sufficient enough to light up the entire neighborhood. So, the remaining siblings, along with their mother, did the only thing they could do; they turned to the Lord and prayed.

Even though everyone was still waiting with bated breath for the telephone call, when the telephone finally did ring, everyone screamed out of sheer nerves! "Michael, you answer that phone," exclaimed an extremely distraught Irene, who looked as though she might wind up in the county hospital herself.

Michael dreaded approaching the phone. “Hello, Dad. How’s Ricky?”

His father simply answered, “Bad, very bad. He’s in extremely critical condition with extensive brain damage to the base of the brain. Tell your mother I’ll be home shortly.”

Michael didn’t need to say a word to his mother. She could read his expression like a detailed map leading to additional trials. Irene screeched louder than anyone had ever heard her scream, as she fell to the floor and assumed the fetal position.

“No, Lord! No, Lord! No, Lord! I just can’t deal with this! Have mercy on me, my Lord, I implore you!”

Michael has never forgotten the image of his mother, curled up in the fetal position on the floor, wailing for divine mercy. It was one of the most sorrowful scenes Michael has ever witnessed in his entire life.

Dick finally arrived home. He took his time as he chose his words with deliberated discretion, relaying the experience at the hospital, but ultimately, there were no good words to share with his wife who was frantically pacing the floor.

Dick continued, “Ironically, Rick has no scars or bruising on his body with the exception of one on his forehead. Apparently, the ski on the snowmobile hit a railroad tie hidden under the fresh, Christmas snow. This caused Rick’s head to snap forward and his forehead to hit the windshield, causing damage to the frontal lobe of the brain. However, the more extreme damage was inflicted to the base, or stem of the brain, due to the sudden snapping action." Dick felt deep compassion for his loved ones as they all listened while shedding tears in the same room where just hours ago, they were celebrating the best Christmas they ever shared.

Rick was on life support systems and the doctor's prognosis was not a favorable one. Dr. Higgins had the unfortunate and painful responsibility of informing Dick and Cassie that Rick was in a constant, vegetative state. The doctor regretfully informed Dick that his namesake would never come out of the coma, but the doctor would not conjecture on how long Rick might survive.

Rick's graduation picture taken just 1 year prior to his accident

Irene simply would not accept this diagnosis. She was more than prepared to wage war with a sword of prayers. She could hardly wait for a decent hour of the morning to arrive so she could enlist all her friends and relatives as soldiers in this war of prayer. Surely, God would honor those prayers and finally grant a miracle, at least in this case. Irene was so exhausted that she looked as though a steam roller had flattened her pale face. The only color on her face was the profuse red from her bloodshot eyes. It seemed to her that she was drowning in a valley of tears!

The entire family was demolished. Michael did not know what he could do for his inconsolable mother, except to solicit prayers. So, Michael and his sister Sharon crisscrossed the entire city, stopping at every church they could find. Michael and Sharon implored prayers for the family, explaining the situation with Rick, John, and Maureen in as succinct a fashion as possible. Michael and Sharon included convents too. They knew they needed as much prayer ammunition as possible for their mother's war!

One of the stops that Sharon and Michael made was to a mission seminary near the O'Brien home. The priest who answered the door was most empathetic. He assured Michael and Sharon that the entire O'Brien family would remain in his prayers, and beyond that, he offered to celebrate a special Mass the following Sunday for Ricky. The priest directed Michael to invite the entire family and friends to attend.

That Sunday finally arrived, and the chapel in the mission seminary was filled beyond capacity. Like creeks overflowing from the warm spring weather melting the winter's snow, the chapel was so crowded that it overflowed out into the long corridors outside the chapel. The priests had never met John and Maureen, and they were all equally astonished at the burden this woman Irene was being asked to carry.

One of the priests in particular, named Ralph, bonded with the O'Brien family. Father Ralph paid frequent visits to the hospital, laying hands on Rick, and praying for a miracle. He was a frequent visitor to the O'Brien house and a guest at many informal dinners for which he required no invitation. This crisis made Father Ralph an honorary member of the O'Brien family.

Rick was eventually taken off life support and could breathe on his own. Dr. Higgins had to caution the family not to find any hope in this situation; the brainwaves were unchanged. Ricky had to receive his nourishment through a feeding tube. Irene's pain was inexpressible through words, but if it's true that a picture tells a thousand words, then the expression on Irene's face belonged in an art museum. There wasn't a more devastating expression that evoked as much sympathy as Irene's expression did, as she gazed upon her helpless son.

Many of her friends, with the very best of intentions, would commend her for being a woman of strong faith, the likes of which they had never met. Irene would react wildly! "I am not strong! I have never felt so powerless and weak in my entire life. I swear, as God is my witness, if one more person refers to me as 'strong,' I just don't know what I'll do." Then Irene would depart, imploring of her friends, "Just pray. Please, just pray."

After four months of lying comatose in the county hospital, Ricky was eventually moved to a Catholic nursing home. The Brothers took excellent care of Ricky and were very cordial to the O'Brien family. As was the case with Ricky's stay in the hospital, family members visited Rick in the nursing home several times a day. It was most taxing on Irene, who had John and Maureen to take care of before she could get out for a visit to the nursing home to pray for her son - the one who wanted to become a member of the United States Marine Corps after graduating from college. It wasn't long before the nursing home became a home-away-from-home for the O'Brien family. Some of the Brothers likewise became an extended family of the O'Briens.

Rick's stay at the nursing home was a tumultuous experience, worse than that of the most daring roller-coaster ride in America. There were times when Rick was close to death, burning with fever, only to be resilient and recover from whatever infection he had acquired. It seemed as though life for the O'Briens had turned into an hourly newsflash of the most recent status of Rick's health.

Irene and Richard were to celebrate their twenty-fifth wedding anniversary that year, but because Ricky was in a coma, neither felt like a celebration. Instead, they marked the occasion quietly with just the immediate family.

One day, the Most Reverend James McNulty, Bishop of Buffalo, was visiting some of the elderly priests in the nursing home. The Bishop passed Rick's room and was taken aback by the age of the young man who occupied the bed; he immediately inquired of the Brothers to explain to him the situation. The Bishop was aware of John and Maureen, but he was not aware of Ricky. He went into Rick's room and prayed for an hour on his knees.

The Bishop then called the O'Briens unexpectedly at their residence. He explained he had experienced an overwhelming presence of the Holy Spirit in Ricky's room; he promised he would be returning in the near future. The Bishop said he would call the O'Brien household in advance of any visit, in the event that any family member was available to join him in prayer. The Bishop kept his promise and payed several visits to Ricky's room, telling Irene on one occasion, "In all my years of priestly ministry, I've never seen a cross so heavy placed on anyone's shoulder." Then, the Bishop embraced Irene.

Bishop McNulty was not the only person to have alleged such an experience of the Holy Spirit while in Rick's room. One day, several young people who went to visit Rick, gave their lives to the Lord before departing the room. One of the young men, addicted to drugs, was freed from his addiction instantaneously and wept as he also surrendered his life to the Lord.

On the morning of August 17, 1972, Ricky died. Ultimately, it was kidney failure that stole his life away. It was the end of a twenty-month long saga. Michael, who had been at the nursing home that morning, called Father Ralph to meet him at the house.

Irene had just finished John and Maureen's dressings and was beginning to prepare them breakfast when Michael and Father Ralph entered the kitchen. Irene was very intuitive and neither Michael nor Father Ralph had to say a word. Irene simply fell into a kitchen chair and wept.

Family members and then friends, were notified. It was decided that Ricky would be waked locally but would be buried in Holy Cross Cemetery in the small town of Ovid. The same cemetery that Irene passed on her walks to and from school as a little girl; a little girl that dreamed of a wonderful life filled with the laughter of a large, happy, healthy family.

At the family's private viewing during the wake, Dick went up to the casket first. He held firmly onto the top of the casket. Then he started sobbing and shaking so hard that the family worried the casket would fall. It was the first time that most of the children ever saw their father cry. Dick was unaware of his surroundings. All he could see was his namesake, Richard William O'Brien III, who was a mere twenty years of age, lifelessly laid out in a casket. There was not a dry eye in the room and the family, including Irene, respectfully allowed Dick to mourn as long as he needed without interruption.

The funeral procession followed Route 90, eventually to Route 96A. The procession made the right hand turn at the blinking signal light onto Main Street in the village of Ovid. It then made a right hand turn onto Gilbert Road as it made its way to the third driveway of Holy Cross Cemetery, where almost to the end of the road, on the left hand side, was an empty grave awaiting the burial of Rick. It was August; there were no tiger lilies, no butterflies, and no cherries left on the trees. Irene's face was void of any expression; she was just stoic. As people approached her to offer their final condolences, most remarked what a strong woman of faith she was and how much they admired her.

Standing at the gravesite alone with Michael, Irene somberly stated, "It's much more painful sending him out of this world than it was bringing him into this world. However, the joy of the birth relieved those pains. What, in God's name, will ever relieve this pain?" Michael embraced his mother.

Holy Cross Cemetery

Irene returned to Buffalo in Father Ralph's car, where she let her guard down. She acknowledged how much she objected to people calling her a strong woman of faith. "Don't they understand how much I hurt? I feel like my life has become a massive tug-of-war in my heart, being pulled from one dreadful situation to the next. There are no winners of this tug-of-war! I'm so exhausted. I have nothing left to give. Every ounce of strength has been drained from me. My soul feels as though it's in the middle of a draught. Why can't people understand that?"

Father Ralph consoled Irene as only he could. Irene trusted his wisdom. "No, Irene, people do not understand. Not because they don't want to understand, but because your walk with the Lord is impossible to comprehend. I can't even begin to imagine the pain you experience, although you wear the pain well, always exuding joy, always serving others." Then Father Ralph added, with special emphasis in the tone of his voice, "There's nothing wrong with feeling weak. It's appropriate that you acknowledge your weakness before the Lord. It only serves to make you rely more fully on Him, knowing that you could never do it independently. In that manner, God alone is glorified. Let's not forget the Scripture verse from Corinthians, 'So, now I am glad to boast of my weaknesses, so the power of God can work through me. His power is made perfect in our weaknesses' (2 Corinthians 12:19).

Chapter Seven

SIMON HELPS JESUS CARRY HIS CROSS

For Irene, Christianity was not merely a religion, it was a relationship. It was a personal relationship with Jesus as her Lord and Savior. However, she also recognized that her Baptism was a baptism into the body of Christ. "For by one Spirit we were all baptized into one body" (I Corinthians 12:13). Further in Corinthians, Paul expounds on this reality, "And if one member suffers, all the members suffer with it; if one member is honored, all the members rejoice with it. Now you are Christ's body, and individually members of it" (I Corinthians 12: 26-27).

Irene was equally familiar with the verse from Ephesians, "And He gave some as apostles, and some as prophets, and some as evangelists, and some as pastors and teachers, for the equipping of the saints for the work of service, to the building up of the body of Christ" (Ephesians 4: 11-12). Therefore, Irene considered her active participation in her church, along with her prayer group, as a mandatory expression of the authenticity of her personal relationship with Jesus. The two could not be exclusive of one another as far as she was concerned. You just could not have a legitimate, personal relationship with the Lord without actively participating as a member of the "body of Christ," according to Irene's theology, undoubtedly passed down from her mother Laura.

Irene often wondered to herself, "What would I ever do without my loving family and my brothers and sisters in the Lord?"

Irene's children always rallied to assist their mother the best they could as they grew older. Michael, with the assistance of his siblings and close friends, sponsored two major fundraisers to purchase electric wheelchairs for John and Maureen, who by now, were completely crippled and unable to walk. The first was a spaghetti dinner held at the mission seminary where Father Ralph abided. Michael secured a popular, local group of singers to provide the entertainment. Tickets sold like wildfire!

The eventful evening was a tremendous success in every regard. The most important component of the success was the joyous time experienced by John and Maureen. They met dozens of new friends who were deeply touched by their life story. Local media attended the event and interviewed John and Maureen. They felt like celebrities as they later watched themselves on all three local networks! Subsequently, they received additional donations in the mail, accompanied by notes assuring them of love and prayers. The notes usually concluded with a comment about what an inspiration they were.

Maureen dresses up for a fundraising extravaganza.

However, additional funds still needed to be raised and this fact was anticipated. Michael sponsored the second event in a much larger venue because John and Maureen were becoming well known throughout Western New York. With the assistance of the local written and televised media, tickets sold even more rapidly than they did for the first event. There now were sufficient funds to purchase the wheelchairs, but this was kept secret from John, Maureen, and Irene. Also, a local car dealership, after watching the television news, donated a wheelchair-lift van. This also was kept secret from the trio.

For John and Maureen, waiting for the evening of the special event was worse than waiting for Christmas! The evening of the gala finally arrived; both John and Maureen were dressed in special gowns sewn specifically for this occasion. When they were pushed into the venue on their regular wheelchairs, their eyes lit up like lanterns when they saw the size of the crowd and realized with appreciation, that everyone in attendance was there for them. As everyone waited for dinner to be served, John and Maureen met scores of new friends who were deeply touched by their presence and their words, as they shared in conversation. They were having a marvelous time!

Things settled down a bit while dinner was being served, with John and Maureen sitting with their brother Michael at the head table. After dinner was complete, Michael, dressed in a tuxedo and serving as the Master of Ceremonies, addressed the crowd and thanked them on behalf of the entire O'Brien family for the support of their presence. Then, he had his two brothers, Stephen and Patrick, bring out the electric wheelchairs. John and Maureen's eyes grew wider than half dollars as tears streamed down their cheeks. Stephen and Patrick carried John and Maureen to their electric wheelchairs as Michael announced, "Due to your love and generosity, John and Maureen are about to self-mobilize for the first time in decades!" The crowd jumped to their feet, friends and strangers alike. They applauded, whistled, and screamed with delight. The venue suddenly sounded like the Beatles arriving at Shea Stadium; it was deafening!

As John and Maureen initially experimented with their electric wheelchairs, it looked more like a demolition derby than anything else. Michael wondered if he should have equipped his brother and sister with helmets as protective gear. With patience and practice, John and Maureen eventually became proficient in navigating themselves about the room. The local media captured it all on tape. They were indeed becoming local celebrities; celebrities that profoundly impacted the lives and faith of thousands of people across Western New York.

Michael holds microphone while John extends his gratitude

No one in that venue was more ecstatic than Irene O'Brien. She wept tears of joy for the delightful expressions on the faces of John and Maureen. The void in her heart from losing her eldest son would never be filled. Irene never experienced a day's relief from the dark void that filled her like a black hole in the outermost regions of the universe. At times, she felt as though the pain of the loss of Ricky would strangle the very life from her. However, tonight she was experiencing the truth contained in the words, "To everything there is a season. A time to weep, and a time to laugh. A time to mourn, and a time to dance" (Ecclesiastes: 3: 4-5).

As Irene looked up, she was astonished to see John and Maureen, for the first time in their life, out on the dance floor, dancing in their new electric wheelchairs! Irene could not adequately thank God for the many new friends, and even many strangers, who had made this possible for her, John, and Maureen. For the time being, at least, it lightened her burden.

With the electric wheelchairs and the wheelchair van, new opportunities presented themselves for John and Maureen. Older siblings and close friends took John and Maureen places they had never been. Stephen and his wife were particularly generous with their time. It was as if the doors to a new world had been opened for them. Patrick was of great assistance. As the youngest O'Brien sibling, Patrick became a patient bondservant to John and Maureen. He frequently assisted with their outings. It was always critical to pay attention to the heat and humidity to protect John and Maureen from dehydrating, but nothing was going to prevent John and Maureen from crossing some new thresholds.

They went to the zoo, the aquarium, a Sabres hockey game, and a Kenny Rogers and Dolly Parton concert. John was even able to attend a Diana Ross concert, where Diana hugged, kissed, and conversed with John in front of a sold out audience of 18,000 fans. Miss Ross had more than passed John's litmus test for a person of character. The pain of John and Maureen's daily dressing routine was no less excruciating, but when they knew that someone had made plans to assist them in escaping the confines of their kitchen chairs, it made all the difference in the world to them, and to Irene. Quite literally, it was like Simon helping Jesus carry his cross.

One of the new friends that Irene, John, and Maureen had acquired was a humble, yet wealthy woman named Helen. John and Maureen simply loved her bright, red Cadillac. They used to comment how impeccably dressed Helen was, no matter what time of the day she visited. John once commented, "I bet she spends three hours in front of the mirror before she even leaves the house." John did not mean this as an insult, but rather as a compliment.

Helen always had her face made up perfectly. There was never so much as a strand of hair ever out of place on Helen's head. She wore the most fragrant perfumes. Her long nails were always impeccably manicured and polished. Helen was fashionably dressed, wearing the most exquisite jewelry. Her delightful sense of humor was what John and Maureen appreciated the most. They were in stitches from the moment of her arrival, to her departure. Nothing filled Irene's heart with deeper joy than to witness John and Maureen's laughter. After all, it was Irene who daily witnessed their painful sobs as the dressings were dutifully changed.

With the new wheelchairs available, Helen invited John and Maureen for an afternoon ride on her yacht. She availed her sons to assist. Patrick also volunteered to assist with his brother and sister. John and Maureen had never been on a boat before, so they were well beyond excited, and a tad bit nervous as the day approached. When they wheeled themselves onto the beautiful yacht, John exclaimed, "This boat is bigger than some houses I've been in!"

Helen's sons and Patrick navigated the yacht, while Helen entertained and fed John and Maureen, all the while assuring they were kept cool. They toured the mighty Niagara River and the waters of Lake Erie; they had a fabulous time, bragging about their experience for weeks to come. John and Maureen deeply appreciated Helen, and Irene appreciated her even more for the gift of laughter she consistently bestowed on John and Maureen. "A time to laugh, a time to cry" (Ecclesiastes 3:4), Irene thought to herself.

The "time to cry" did not take long to arrive on the clock of life for the O'Brien family. It was a hot, humid, summer day. The boys' room had a window air conditioner that was turned on high to seek refuge from the assaulting humidity. The boys were relaxing and watching television while they were being kept cool. Suddenly, the circuit breaker tripped, so Stephen ran down in the basement to reset it. Michael had all of his college notebooks beneath the air conditioner and these papers served as fodder for an electrical fire. The fire spread rapidly, and the house had to be immediately evacuated. The sound of sirens was still off in the distance as dancing flames were engulfing the roof. The firefighters finally arrived and immediately went to work. There was considerable damage to the house from the fire, the smoke, and the water.

Although Irene and Dick realized that the most important thing was that everyone had escaped without injury, Irene was simply stunned as she watched her home, unbelievably, being consumed by flames. *Lord, it has just been a year since you took my son Ricky home. Now this! How much more can I bear, Lord? I'm only a mere mortal. Where are we supposed to go now?*

Father Ralph arrived on the scene. Much like "Simon," he lightened Irene's burden by informing her and Dick that the family could stay at the mission seminary. There were sufficient empty rooms, equipped with private baths, and plenty of fresh food. Irene just fell into Father Ralph's arms and cried on his shoulder, as her husband held her hand. For the first time, Father Ralph was at a loss for words, as he just patted Irene on the back and witnessed the house going up in flames.

As it turned out, many of the O'Briens moved into the mission seminary. Irene and Dick were extremely grateful for the shelter and food, as well as adequate accommodations to do John and Maureen's daily dressings. John and Maureen embraced the change of scenery. Construction workers got busy repairing the house; Dick and his sons helped salvage precious items from the house. When the new drywall was finally in place, Dick and the boys painted the entire house. Finally, after approximately four weeks of being displaced, the O'Briens moved back into the house. "How many times can lightning hit the same place?" Irene silently thought to herself.

Eventually, Irene was blessed to become a grandmother. Nothing, absolutely nothing, and no one, delighted Irene more than her grandchildren did. She adored her grandchildren and the feeling was mutual; they all loved their "Grandma Rene." If anyone could lift Irene's spirits, as well as those of John and Maureen, it was the grandchildren. They were very good to their Uncle John, Aunt Maureen, and their Grandma Rene. Each of the grandchildren, in their own unique manner, were definitely "Simon" who helped carry the cross by the genuine love and concern they expressed on each visit. Irene was also immensely proud of her own children in their roles as parents. She loved to chat about her children and grandchildren with friends, and naturally, she always had the most recent photographs to proudly display.

Father Ralph was visiting the O'Brien household for dinner one evening. During the dinner conversation, Father Ralph mentioned that he would be vacationing in Italy to visit his parents. Ralph and Dick became very engaged in a discussion about Italy, as Richard had served in Italy during World War II and commented on how much he loved the country.

Richard expressed, "That's the one place I always wanted to return and visit."

The reason he had not visited Italy was obvious, he and his wife had long ago laid down their lives for the intricate care of John and Maureen. Dick and Irene never complained, but nonetheless, they had never been able to vacation alone together since their honeymoon in Lake George, nearly twenty-six years ago!

Irene chimed in on the conversation. She expressed with definite certitude, "If I were ever able to travel to one place, just one place, it would be my homeland, Ireland. I think it would be so fascinating to visit County Cork and County Clare, and explore where my relatives lived. I'd love to visit the churches where they were baptized. I think it would be an unimaginable dream to find one of the old homesteads and walk the grounds. That's what I ardently wish I could do. Not that I wouldn't love Italy, Father Ralph, don't misunderstand me but I've always dreamed of discovering my ancestors' homestead!"

Dick was more cynical about Ireland and added, "If you ever go over there, the Irish will tell you everything they think you want to hear. They'll tell you what wonderful folks your ancestors were, how they daily walked together to church, and where they lounged at the local pubs. As long as you're listening, they'll keep talking. You know, I'm convinced there is a measure of truth to Irish blarney," concluded Richard. Ralph and Irene had a hearty laugh over Richard's cynicism.

Then Father Ralph shocked Irene and Dick with an invitation to join him. "Listen, you both could stay with me at my parents. They would love to meet you! We also have several missions in Ireland where we could stay expense-free. To satisfy you both, we could spend one week in Italy and then the concluding week in Ireland. You've been married twenty-six years and have traveled nowhere alone. You couldn't celebrate your twenty-fifth anniversary last year because Ricky was still in a coma. This excursion could be considered a delayed twenty-fifth wedding anniversary celebration. All you'd have to pay for is your airfare. My parents and fellow priests would take excellent care of the rest. I think we'd have the adventure of a lifetime," concluded Father Ralph, with genuine, high-pitched excitement in his voice.

Richard was silent. In his heart, he was saying, "Let's go!" Yet Dick understood the predicament of caring for John and Maureen. He waited for Irene to speak.

"Father Ralph, there's nothing I would love to do more than meet your parents, tour Italy with Richard, and visit my homeland, but I have no one to care for John and Maureen," lamented Irene.

"Isn't there anyone?" inquired a heart-broken Father Ralph.

"No, there's no one. I've had a couple people volunteer in the past, and they landed on the floor. I arrive at the hospital in the wee hours of the morning to finish their dressings before the transfusions. If the dressings aren't correctly completed, John and Maureen will suffer additionally. I can't subject them to that," explained Irene.

As Father Ralph stood up to leave, he announced, "I'm going to pray fervently that the Lord sends you someone you can fully trust to care for John and Maureen for those two weeks!"

Irene, guarding her heart against disappointment, said to Father Ralph, "Well, you just go ahead and pray, and do me a favor: Let me be the first to know when the Lord answers your prayers!"

The next afternoon, Helen stopped by for a visit, looking more glamorous than ever. Irene, John, and Maureen relayed the story of Father Ralph's invitation to travel overseas with him. Helen, who had been fortunate enough to travel all over the world, inquired with a tone of excitement, "Well, are you going?"

Irene responded, "Helen, you know the answer to that question. I have no one to care for John and Maureen."

"You have me!" Helen exclaimed.

John and Maureen laughed hysterically. The last person on the face of the earth they could imagine surviving the process of doing their dressings was the forever glamorous Helen. Irene graciously thanked Helen for the generous offer, but repeated the incidents where other good-natured souls had also volunteered but could not persevere. Irene added, "If the dressings aren't done with exact precision, then John and Maureen suffer more extensively during the day as bandages slip, causing new blisters."

Helen became extremely stubborn. "At least give me the opportunity to prove myself! I want you and Dick to go; you deserve the vacation and I believe the timing is just perfect. You can train me, Irene, and then give me the chance to go solo as you carefully watch over me. There's no harm in trying. I insist! Expect to see me early tomorrow for my first lesson!" exclaimed an enthused and confident Helen.

"Are you serious?" asked a stunned Irene.

Helen wasted no time in responding, "I've never been more serious about anything in my entire life! You and Dick are going on this vacation. This is the Lord opening a door and you are going to walk through that door before it closes. Get your passports ready."

The next morning, the bright, red Cadillac pulled into the O'Brien driveway. An almost unrecognizable Helen emerged from the car wearing denim jeans and a navy sweatshirt. Helen's hair was pulled back in a ponytail and she wore no makeup or jewelry except her wedding ring. It was very apparent that Helen was determined to win Irene's confidence and she was going to rely on the Lord for the strength to accomplish her mission. Just like the old adage says, "You can't judge a book by its cover," it was about to become true that you also can't judge a "Simon" by her makeup and jewelry!

Helen marched up the stairs with her head held high and her shoulders drawn back, and entered John and Maureen's bedroom. "Let the games begin!" Helen proclaimed in her typical humorous style that enamored John and Maureen so deeply. Helen studied Irene as she methodically removed one bandage at a time from Maureen's frail body until Maureen was naked. Helen had previously only seen Maureen dressed in her gowns. Helen had no idea that Maureen's body was so severely covered with blisters resembling third-degree burns. It broke Helen's heart to witness Maureen squirm and cry, but Helen never winced, not even once. She watched intently as Irene washed and redressed Maureen, feeling astounded that Irene had done this for so many years without a whisper of complaint. Irene was amazed that Helen made it through the first day of training, as were John and Maureen.

The day finally arrived for Helen to fly solo. Helen completed Maureen and John's dressings without a word of assistance from Irene. "Well, did I pass the test? Do I live up to your standards? Have I gained your confidence?" inquired an enthusiastic Helen.

"You more than passed the test, Helen!" exclaimed Irene. "You are an absolute angel! In fact, you remind me of the passage about 'entertaining angels unaware,' (Hebrews 13:2). I will tell you this much, you unequivocally are the answer to Father Ralph's prayers."

So it came to pass that Richard, Irene, and Father Ralph began planning their trip. The three comrades would sit at the kitchen table with maps and calendars, as John and Maureen looked on, sharing in the excitement. Irene could not believe this was happening to her! After twenty-six years of marriage, she finally was being granted the time to be alone with her husband, not to mention that they would be visiting their homeland together. Irene could not have been happier.

The day of departure finally arrived. As many of the O'Brien family members as were available, met their parents at the airport. They wanted to share in the joy and excitement and wish everyone a safe trip. The children marveled that at last, with their mother fifty-three years of age, their father fifty-two years, and having been married for over twenty-six years, their parents were actually being afforded the opportunity of a vacation together!

Irene and Dick in Ireland. 'Bridge Over Troubled Waters?'

Chapter Eight

UNTIL DEATH DO US PART

Everything was going fabulously well with Helen's perfect execution of completing John and Maureen's dressings without a flaw. The reality was that John and Maureen tremendously enjoyed the presence of Helen. She always found a way to make them laugh. She spoiled them rotten, planning several excursions during the day for their enjoyment.

A couple of long-distance phone calls were placed, by a typically nervous Irene, to check on things at home, but Irene's nervousness was quickly quelled when she listened to the tone in John and Maureen's voices. Irene had learned long ago to decipher problems and concerns by listening attentively to John and Maureen's tone of voice, rather than merely their words alone. It was as if Irene had cracked a secret code. Helen was relentless in reassuring Irene that all was well, and insisted that she just relax and enjoy herself. She promised Irene a night out upon her return home, so that she could hear all the exciting details of the trip. Helen was truly a dear friend and a blessing from heaven above. Dick always experienced a sense of relief as Irene communicated the good news from home.

Postcards arrived in the mail for the other children. Each postcard noted that their parents were having a grand time. Some of the siblings banded together to complete chores that they knew their mother would deeply appreciate upon her return home. The basement was cleaned meticulously, as was the garage. Two cars would now actually be able to fit into the garage. A couple of rooms in the house received a fresh coat of paint. The carpets were steam-cleaned and the hardwood floors were polished. As the time of their return home drew closer, fresh flowers were placed on the dining room table and in their parent's bedroom to cheer them up just a bit. The house looked beautiful and was so spotlessly clean that it would pass the white glove test. "Mr. Clean" couldn't hold a candle to this O'Brien Clan who adored their parents.

The flight home had a layover at JFK International Airport. Irene called home to confirm that the connecting flight to Buffalo was scheduled to leave on time. Irene mentioned to Michael, in a desperate tone, "Please pray for your father; he has a terrible cold and cough. I think the dampness in Ireland was just too much for him. We had misty showers every day we were in Ireland. I guess that's why the island is so green." Michael tried to conceal his concern and assured his mother that he would begin to pray and would call members of the prayer group to pray also.

The family was at the airport early to be sure they would not miss the opportunity to welcome their parents home. They had painted a conspicuously large sign that simply read, "Welcome Home." They also decorated the sign with bright green shamrocks of all sizes; Patrick added a pot of gold under a rainbow. The children were most desirous to hear the highlights of their parent's trip. They had a platter of food waiting on the kitchen table so they could break bread as they conversed. Everyone wondered if Irene had actually found an ancestor's homestead. They were bursting at the seams in anticipation of hearing all the details of this once-in-a-lifetime vacation for their parents. The children also could not wait to see the expression on their parent's faces when they saw the fruit of their collective labor, that transformed the house and completed all the chores Irene had been requesting to be accomplished for the past several months.

However, when their parents were ultimately greeted, Irene looked appreciative but also absolutely distraught. She managed to thank everyone for their warm welcome and acknowledged the sign with what appeared to be a forced, weary smile. Dick looked exasperated and had a deep hacking cough that made it difficult for him to speak.

Michael immediately grabbed his father's small, carry-on luggage and inquired, "Dad, are you okay?"

Irene chided, "I told you he developed a bad cold the last couple of days in the dampness of Ireland. He needs to get home and into bed immediately, then he'll be fine."

Michael drove the car home with his father as a passenger. The coughing was incessant and producing sputum. His father could hardly speak, even to answer a simple question. Michael knew this was more than a simple cold that a good night's rest would cure. He feared his father had pneumonia and might need to be taken to the hospital.

The clearest evidence of Irene's deeply rooted concerns regarding her husband's health was the fact that she was oblivious to all that had been accomplished in the house. That was not Irene. Additionally, she had no appetite for the platter on the kitchen table even though it deliberately contained some of her favorite delicacies. She never recognized the fresh flowers on the dining room table. It was further apparent that she was in no mood to discuss the details of the adventurous trip. The children were most understanding and were, quite frankly, as concerned about their father's health as she was.

That night, no one slept at the O'Brien house. Their father coughed and coughed throughout the night. Everyone was gravely concerned and convinced their father had pneumonia. It was decided by 2:00 a.m. that Dick would be taken to the emergency room at the break of dawn. Dick offered no resistance to the prospect.

Sharon took her father to the emergency room in the morning, vowing to call home when there was any news to share. Hours passed and finally the telephone rang; Michael answered it. Sharon's voice was quivering as she requested that Michael come to the hospital immediately for moral support. Signs were not looking the least bit favorable as test results were coming back. He rushed out the door immediately and headed to the hospital.

Michael and Sharon, who just a couple of years earlier, had crossed the city desperately imploring prayers for their injured brother Ricky, were together again facing an ominous situation. Finally, the doctor called them into an office. The tall doctor, with long, wavy, salt and pepper hair, kept pacing the floor as he struggled to find the appropriate words for them.

The doctor finally spoke, "We're going to have to admit your father to the hospital. I know you've informed me that he just returned from a two-week vacation in Europe. I heard you say your father hasn't missed a day of work in ages. I don't doubt you, when I tell you that I find that to be quite incredulous. Your father, well, there's just no easy way to say this: Your father has terminal lung cancer. Both of his lungs are filled with cancer and it's just impossible for me to imagine how he has had the capacity to work the past six months, let alone travel to Europe for the past two weeks. I can't fathom how he was able to do this."

Sharon and Michael turned as white and as cold as a notorious Buffalo blizzard in the middle of January. With their voices trembling like the cowardly lion from *The Wizard of Oz*, they asked the doctor, "What can you do for him?"

The doctor painfully and reluctantly replied, "Unfortunately, there is absolutely nothing we can do for your father except make him as comfortable as we can. He's well beyond receiving any benefits from radiation or chemotherapy treatments. I'm so sorry to have to inform you of this devastating news. I am truly sorry for you and your family."

The doctor sounded very sincere as he spoke those fatal words, but to Sharon and Michael, the words were like bullets leaving the barrel of a shotgun, inflicting deep wounds. They were both in a state of shock and could not believe this was happening to their family. Just one year ago, the house went up in flames. Two years ago, their brother had died after spending nearly two years comatose. Now this! Sharon and Michael felt as though they were so wounded they did not have sufficient strength to stand up from their chairs.

Finally, Sharon summoned enough courage to ask the question that she feared the most. "How long does my father have to live, Doctor?" Sharon and Michael listened intently for the doctor's response like a misbehaved child waits to learn of his punishment - with complete dread.

Visible pain filled the doctor's eyes as his brows lowered and he replied, "Your father has about one month to live."

Bullseye! That was the fatal blow that knocked Sharon and Michael from their chairs. This was surreal; it just could not possibly be happening. Their parents just returned from the first vacation of their married lives and their father only has a month to live. How intolerable! Sharon then requested the answer to another question, "Does my father know of his diagnosis and prognosis?"

The doctor replied, "I wanted to leave that up to you. I can most certainly inform him, however, sometimes it's better coming from family members." The doctor patiently looked on without the whisper of an interruption. Both Michael and Sharon knew, unquestionably, that their father deserved to hear this news from his family. They held a heartfelt, deep conviction that they owed their father that much respect after the life-long sacrifices he made for them.

"Doctor, we'll inform our father. Has he been assigned a room yet?"

"Yes," the doctor replied. "He's in a private room on the third floor; Room 332 to be precise. He's already being administered some pain medication intravenously, so I'm not sure how lucid you'll find him."

Michael and Sharon took the stairs to the third floor, instead of the elevator. They were in no hurry to face this devastating task, definitely one of the most challenging of their lives. Finally, they reached the third floor and found room 332. They saw that their father was wearing an oxygen mask across his nose and they also noticed the intravenous drip of pain medicine.

Dick recognized both his children and motioned them to come into the room. After some small talk about how he was doing, his children informed him that the cause of his hacking cough was lung cancer. Dick assured his children that everything would be fine by saying, "So, they remove the cancerous lung; I have two lungs and all will be fine."

Michael and Sharon looked at each other speechlessly. They felt as though someone had torn the heart out of them. Sharon grasped her father's hand tenderly in hers, while Michael pressed his leg firmly.

"No, Dad, you don't understand. You have advanced cancer in both lungs and there are no treatments available for you," Sharon compassionately informed her father.

With a stoic look on the face of this World War II veteran, Dick removed his oxygen mask and replied, "Then take me home. I want to die in my own home!" Michael and Sharon promised to consult with the doctor regarding that request.

The two siblings lingered with their father for another good hour, as they witnessed his slow absorption of the news they had just shared. Dick then directed them to return home and inform their mother. Michael and Sharon obeyed their father, kissing him goodbye and promising to return. As they were leaving the hospital, they crossed paths with the doctor. They inquired about the feasibility of their father coming home.

The doctor advised, “That would be too much of a burden. Your father needs oxygen and pain medicine.”

Michael asked his sister, “Have we already seen Dad in the house for the last time without knowing it?”

Sharon replied, “That’s the way it happened with Ricky that fateful Christmas!”

As Michael and Sharon arrived home, an anxious Irene was waiting at the opened front door. She looked like a dead person who just had not fallen over yet. Irene read the faces of Michael and Sharon as soon as they stepped out of the car, and then Irene disappeared, quickly retreating into the house.

Before Michael or Sharon could even speak, Irene choked up with heartfelt sobs imploring, “No! No! Don’t tell me. Please, don’t tell me!” As Irene fell into one of the living room chairs, Michael retrieved a box of tissue for his mother. Irene cried out to the Lord, respectfully asking that He remove her from the fiery furnace she felt was consuming her. “Please, Lord. The flames are too hot! Soon there will be nothing left of me.”

Michael and Sharon began calling other members of the family who rushed home to help console their mother. John and Maureen, as well as Patrick, who was only twelve, were crying in disbelief. As Irene began to compose herself, she got on the telephone and began calling friends to pray for Dick, specifically to pray for a miracle. Those friends began calling other friends, until hundreds of people were praying for Dick.

Irene finally went to the hospital to visit her husband of twenty-six years. It pained Irene to see him with the oxygen mask and the intravenous drip. She knew she had to be strong for her husband, but she just found that to be an impossible proposition. Irene sobbed as she leaned over and kissed Richard on the lips. "Oh, Richard, we had such a wonderful time in Europe. You saw your Italy and I saw my Ireland. I'll treasure our time together for eternity! It was the best two weeks of my entire life. I enjoyed you so much, being able to spend every day and all day with the one I love more than anyone else in the world. I thank the Lord for Father Ralph and Helen for making it all possible. God's timing was perfect as it always is. I don't want you to worry; you're being bombarded with prayers. It's about time we had a miracle in this family!"

Irene remained with her husband until she noticed the pain medicine was putting him to sleep. All the other family members developed a rotation schedule to assure their father always had someone in the room. As the third week of Dick's stay in the hospital was concluding, Michael and Sharon happened to be visiting. Their father commissioned them to get him out of the hospital immediately. Dick's wish was to die at home surrounded by his family.

Sounding like a commanding officer in the United States Air Force, Richard ordered, "As my eldest daughter and eldest surviving son, I depend on you to get me out of here today!"

Michael and Sharon wasted no time. They found the doctor and insisted their father was going home as per his wishes. "I will not deny his request," asserted Sharon.

"Is there anyone at home skilled enough to give him an injection every six hours around the clock?" inquired the doctor.

"I'll gladly do that for my father," affirmed Michael.

The doctor reluctantly conceded, as if he even had a choice. He ordered two oxygen tanks to be delivered to the house immediately. One tank for the upstairs bedroom and one tank downstairs. The doctor then retrieved a box of medicated syringes and instructed Michael how to utilize them. That day, a Tuesday, Richard returned to his home and family. It reminded him of returning to the States after completing his combat duty in the Air Force. Although he was ecstatic to be home with the ones he loved, Dick knew that the biggest battle of his life yet awaited him.

Tuesday, July 2, 1974, exactly one week since Dick had come home from the hospital, Irene became a widow at the young age of fifty-three. Michael had come downstairs for the 6:00 a.m. injection. Richard was laying on the couch, obviously close to death. Michael alerted the family and each had their last words with their Dad.

Michael carried John out to say his final goodbye. All John could mutter through his tears was, "I love you, Dad!" Was there anything more that could be said?

Next, Michael carried Maureen out for her final words. Maureen was sobbing uncontrollably, "I love you, Daddy. When you get to heaven, please ask Jesus to send us a miracle! Please, Daddy. Please ask Jesus to send us a miracle!"

The last to say goodbye was his wife. Irene, gently stroking Dick's forehead and cheeks with the back of her hand, simply and sweetly told her husband, "I have loved you with my whole heart as I promised I would until death do us part. We've had some rough times, but we always had each other to make it through those rough times. What will I ever do without you, Dick? What will I ever do? In our entire marriage, I have never enjoyed you more than I have these past weeks; particularly this last week. I so thoroughly enjoyed having you home and caring for you, since you have taken such good care of me my entire life."

Richard drew his final breath. Irene laid across his body. Michael got up to turn off the oxygen tank. To Michael, it was as though he was cutting off the lifeline to the entire household and to the family's future. From his perspective, Michael watched as a young Patrick was punching the kitchen walls. Stephen quickly rushed to Patrick's side and embraced him tightly.

The funeral was packed without an empty seat in the church. Father Ralph was the main celebrant. As the Mass concluded, Richard's casket was slowly carried down the main aisle of the church. Directly behind the casket, John and Maureen were being pushed in their wheelchairs by Patrick and a nephew. Next, Stephen and Michael flanked Irene, holding her up by her elbows to prevent her from collapsing. Michael wondered what was on his mother's mind as she looked at the casket and the two wheelchairs. Undoubtedly, she was asking the Lord how she would ever find the strength to care for John and Maureen without the support of her soulmate. The rest of the family followed the casket out of the church.

The funeral cortege proceeded on Route 90 until it eventually reached Route 96A. It came to the blinking light and turned right onto Main Street in Ovid, until it reached Gilbert Road. It made a right turn onto Gilbert Road and then turned left into the third driveway of Holy Cross Cemetery. Almost to the end of the drive, there on left side, was a grave awaiting the burial of Richard William O'Brien II, next to his son, Richard William O'Brien III.

It was early July. Gilbert Road was flourishing with enormous, beautiful tiger lilies; the colorful butterflies could not be counted; the trees were ripe with cherries. The farmer's field across the road was filled with corn that was already "knee high." Surely, the fireflies would be lighting up the bushes and brush of the Gilbert House, just down the road, later that evening.

Irene reminisced about the days when she was a little girl, in this same area of the cemetery, dreaming of a future filled with the happiness of a good marriage and a house filled with the laughter of many, healthy children. She even recounted that terribly cold day in January 1934 and wondered where all the time had gone. Irene remembered how the anticipation of the future glory of summer used to motivate her to face those bitter, winter days.

Chapter Nine

THE GOLDEN RULE

Irene missed Dick more than words could express, but it was not her nature to implode. She affirmed the validity that it was in her weakness that the power of God was made perfect. Irene had the grace to focus on the needs of others, often placing them above her own.

When Irene learned that a friend had someone in their family pass, she would be present to express her sympathy. However, she expressed her sympathy not merely with words, she would deliver the family a meal. A meal prepared by Irene O'Brien on such occasions consisted of a roasted turkey, a baked ham, a roast of beef, mashed potatoes with vegetables, and several pies for dessert. Experience had taught Irene how exhausted a family is returning from a wake. She also remembered the throng of friends and relatives that would tag along to the house. She wanted to assure there would be plenty of food. She became well known for such thoughtfulness and generosity. In fact, it was Irene who started a "bereavement committee" in her parish, and she served the families of strangers as generously as she served the best of her friends.

Michael was notorious for bringing homeless people to his mother's house. Irene never scolded him. When the homeless person awoke from a comfortable night's sleep, Irene dressed the kitchen table with her best china as though she were serving the Lord himself. She cooked omelets, pancakes, toast, and served sliced cantaloupe. She conversed with the stranger during breakfast and then packed them a hearty lunch. Michael would then return the homeless person to a shelter.

There was a dear friend of Irene who lost her three-year-old daughter in a backyard swimming pool accident. This friend had a son the exact age as Patrick. Since Irene's friend was suffering such deep depression at the loss of her daughter, Irene volunteered to take that son into her own home. The friend was most grateful. So it came to pass that the adolescent, young man moved into the O'Brien household. He and Patrick became best friends, after all, they both had tragically lost a sibling. Irene seized every opportunity to listen empathetically to the friend. She would then share the tenets of her faith, a faith that not just "talked the talk," but most definitely "walked the walk." The young man acquired a deep respect for Irene. When the young man returned home, he eventually entered the seminary.

Irene would be quick to visit any friend that was in the hospital and pray with them. On one occasion, she was visiting a friend who was admitted for an extended stay. Irene managed to visit almost daily. During her visits, she noticed that a gentleman across the hall never seemed to have any visitors. The friend explained to Irene that the man was terminal and had no family. Irene began visiting the man and praying with him. She continued to visit the man even after her friend was discharged from the hospital. Every day she visited and prayed with the man, who was eventually converted to Christianity.

One day, upon arriving at the hospital, Irene was informed that the gentleman had passed and was, just moments earlier, removed from the room. Irene inquired regarding the whereabouts of the man's remains.

A doctor told Irene, "His body is in the hospital morgue. We'll momentarily be calling the university to dispose of it. The poor man had no family."

"Had no family?!" exclaimed Irene, "Well, I'm his sister! Don't send that body away until I call the funeral parlor," Irene adamantly insisted. She then went to the nearest phone and called the funeral home that had taken care of her son and husband.

"Anthony, this is Irene O'Brien. There's a gentleman I've been visiting in the hospital for a month. He became a Christian during that time. The gentleman has no family but his brothers and sisters in the Lord. I want you to pick up his body and a hold a wake tomorrow evening, and then bury him the next day. He isn't a Catholic, but he deserves a Christian burial."

Anthony deeply respected Irene O'Brien as a genuine woman of God. He merely inquired, "Irene, if he has no family, why are we having a wake?"

Irene responded with haste, "You let me worry about that, just send someone over immediately to retrieve the body and have him ready for a wake by 6:00 p.m. tomorrow evening." Irene hung up the phone and rushed to find the doctor. She informed him that the funeral director was en route to claim the body.

Irene arrived home and began calling her friends to brief them of the situation. Irene requested that each friend meet her at the funeral home for a prayer service. She further directed each friend she spoke with to call at least one other person. When the wake was held, over one hundred brothers and sisters in the Lord were in attendance.

Anthony approached Irene and sighed, "Irene O'Brien, you are a remarkable woman!"

She replied, "There's nothing remarkable about this. It's just a simple illustration of the Golden Rule, 'Do unto others as you would have others do unto you' " (Matthew 7:12). Then Irene inquired what time the burial would be the next day and at which cemetery. Anthony shared the relevant information. She stated assuredly, "Don't you worry, Anthony. We'll be at the cemetery tomorrow." On a day filled with mud from teaming torrents of rain, fifty people showed up to bury their new "brother in the Lord."

There was an occasion when an elderly senior, who was a shut in, called Irene for prayers because she had been feeling ill for days and was running a fever. She could not get to a doctor, nor could she afford any unnecessary medical bills. Irene, without a second thought, said, "Not to worry, I'm on my way over," and hung up the phone. She got into her old Toyota and immediately drove over to the friend's house.

Irene gave her friend an alcohol rubdown to lower the fever. Then, she prepared some soup and toast for her friend, along with a tall glass of juice. Irene sat in the bedroom and visited and prayed for an hour before departing. The next day, she stopped in to check on her friend; her fever was gone and she was feeling fine. The friend could not have been more grateful.

Irene came to enjoy the simple things in life. She loved spending time with her children and grandchildren. Realizing how fast time was passing, she cherished every moment she spent with her family. There were absolutely no limits to her love for them.

When John was suffering from a deep depression after the loss of his father, Sharon suggested to her mother that they rent a Winnebago, and take her three children, along with John, Maureen, and Patrick, on a trip across the country. Sharon was convinced that this would give John something to look forward to. Irene couldn't imagine how two ladies, one of them a senior, could accomplish such a task, but she agreed immediately with Sharon that it would do John a world of good.

Sharon and Irene poured over maps at the kitchen table, showing John all the exciting places they would visit. John's spirits lifted. All was fine until the day Sharon pulled the Winnebago into the driveway. Irene took one look at the monstrous vehicle and almost swallowed her tongue! "Sharon, you and I are going to cross the Rocky Mountains driving that thing?!" Irene only needed to think of John and soon they were all on their way.

In 1982, Irene received an invitation to attend a private function with Mother Teresa of Calcutta. John and Maureen were included in the invitation. For Irene, Mother Teresa epitomized the Golden Rule. Mother Teresa fell to her knees upon meeting John and Maureen. She placed her head on their laps and implored their prayers; Irene was deeply moved by this scene.

Mother Teresa had been transported to the area on the private jet of a CEO from Cleveland. His wife accompanied Mother Teresa on the flight to and from Cleveland. The couple owned a summer home on the lower Niagara River, not far from Buffalo. Mother Teresa commissioned the wife of the CEO to investigate the two children she met in the wheelchairs, along with their mother, and assure them of her constant prayers. The wife, whose name was Jeanne, did as Mother Teresa instructed. It was not difficult for Jeanne to track down John and Maureen as they had previously received some publicity.

While her husband was a CEO, Jeanne was a playwright. After meeting the O'Brien family, she decided to write a play about John and Maureen and their mother. She was impressed with how completely Irene lived the Golden Rule while tending to the demands of caring for John and Maureen. The play opened in Cleveland, Ohio, with busloads of Western New Yorkers departing from a local mall to attend opening night. The play eventually opened at Rockwell Hall, a theatre at a local college. Finally, the play was videotaped and shown on a television cable station. John and Maureen were beginning to realize that their lives were influencing thousands of other lives; it gave them a sense of purpose.

The pinnacle of Irene's living the Golden Rule was, of course, the care she provided for John and Maureen. They were getting older and their condition was becoming more crippling and more devastating than ever. Irene was also getting older and finding the demands more strenuous. Hospital stays were becoming more frequent. It was during one of these hospital visits that John and Maureen met the newly installed Bishop of Buffalo, the Most Reverend Bishop Edward Head. Bishop Head towered over his predecessor, and John was immediately impressed with his stature.

The Bishop would visit John and Maureen each time they were hospitalized. Irene was astonished when one day,

John blurted out the words, "Bishop Head, my birthday is coming up soon. Would you like to say my home Mass?" The Bishop pulled out his busy schedule, and made a promise to John that he would be honored to celebrate the Mass. Irene wanted to strangle John! The problem was, John invited so many people, they would never fit into the house. The celebration had to be moved to the local parish.

Bishop Head was overwhelmed by the multitude of trials that Irene had endured throughout her life, and yet somehow was able to exude such joy as she was so quick to reach out to any person in need. The Bishop ironically repeated the same words his predecessor had once spoken to Irene, "In all my years of priestly ministry, I have never seen a heavier cross placed upon someone's shoulder." Irene was reminded of how it was her weakness that allowed the Lord's power to be perfected within her.

It was Bishop Head who contacted Catholic Charities and Social Services to successfully solicit some assistance for Irene in terms of having nurses assigned to do the dressings. John and Maureen were blessed to have met some wonderful nurses and nurses aides.

Multitudes of people came to recognize and respect Irene O'Brien as a person who was a perfect example of someone who daily lived and breathed the Golden Rule. Whenever Irene contemplated this, her focus always centered on the word "golden." She understood the true significance of the phrase rested with that singular word. She thought of the relevant scripture, "that the proof of your faith, being more precious than gold which is perishable, even though tested by fire, may be found to result in praise and glory and honor at the revelation of Jesus Christ" (I Peter 1:7).

Chapter 10
THE PIETA

Michael stopped by his mother's house one morning to check on everyone and pay a visit. Irene was still upstairs completing John and Maureen's dressings. After calling up the stairs to announce his presence, Michael pulled some left-overs from the refrigerator and sat at the kitchen table patiently waiting for John and Maureen to come downstairs. Michael then heard his mother's raised voice requesting his presence upstairs.

As Michael walked into John and Maureen's bedroom, he saw that Maureen's body was undressed and was being washed. Irene called him to come closer to the bed. "Do you see this white spot on Maureen's back?" inquired an anxious Irene. Michael drew himself even closer and did, in fact, notice that in the center of Maureen's raw, red back was a small, white spot. "Michael, what do you think that is? Do you think it's some new skin growing in?" his mother asked nervously.

Michael hadn't the faintest idea what the spot could be. He respectfully responded to his mother in a tone that would not alarm John or Maureen. "I see the spot you're talking about. It could well be some new skin attempting to grow. However, I'm not a doctor, Mother," answered Michael.

Irene sighed and responded, "I do think it's a section of healing skin. I'll keep my eyes on it before calling the doctor."

Michael remained in the bedroom and visited with his family while the dressings were being completed. John and Maureen always loved company and bombarded Michael with questions touching upon every subject of life. Because he was a member of a prayer group, John and Maureen perceived Michael to be somewhat of a spiritual advisor and confidant. When the dressings were finished, he assisted in getting them down the stairs to their assigned chairs in the kitchen, then stayed to visit for about an hour. As Michael pulled out of the driveway, he kept the image of that single, white spot on Maureen's back in the forefront of his mind. *Would lightning strike this house again?*

As time passed, that little, white spot was growing larger and other white spots were beginning to appear among the surrounding, blistering, red skin. Whether this was good news that areas of Maureen's most sensitive skin were beginning to heal over, or it was an unknown problem, was not clear. Irene decided to call the doctor, who made a home visit to examine Maureen. Maureen was extremely nervous as she possessed such a sensitive spirit. She shed a gallon of frightened tears as the doctor examined her frail body.

The doctor knew precisely how to deal with Maureen, and he was as gentle and patient as he possibly could be with her. He confessed that he felt inadequate to make a diagnosis. He then highly recommended that Maureen be seen by a specialist who had experience with DEB patients and who, fortunately, was currently working in a hospital in nearby Rochester, New York. This naturally made Irene upset. She called members of the parish and of the prayer group to immediately begin praying for Maureen.

An appointment was hastily made with the doctor in Rochester. Irene could not bring herself to go. She was beginning to suffer from a heart condition and she did not feel she could deal with the stress. Therefore, Michael and Sharon made the hour long drive with Maureen to the hospital in Rochester.

They did not need to wait long to seen by the doctor. Their first impression of this specialist was extremely favorable; he was kind and gentle. He engaged a frightened Maureen in several minutes of pleasant conversation before he politely asked her if he had her permission to examine her body. She reluctantly nodded her head in an affirmative gesture. He knelt down on his knees, promising Maureen he would do his absolute best not to inflict any pain. Then the doctor began methodically removing one bandage at a time. The doctor complimented Maureen's mother for the extraordinary job she did in caring for her. The doctor would stop intermittently to inquire if she was doing okay. Michael and Sharon were astonished at the skillful and compassionate bedside manner of this doctor, feeling as though they were in the presence of Jesus Himself!

The doctor took his time thoroughly examining Maureen's entire fragile body. Then he began to slowly redress Maureen and replace her gown. The doctor gently questioned Maureen if she would mind if he spent a few minutes alone with her siblings. She bravely conceded that she would not mind.

In the privacy his office, the doctor was as gentle with Michael and Sharon as he had been with Maureen. He inquired as to Maureen's age.

Michael responded, "Maureen is twenty-six and will turn twenty-seven come February."

The doctor empathetically continued his conversation by stating, "We have come to learn that the longer DEB patients survive, the greater the risk they will develop squamous cell carcinoma. I don't even find it necessary to put Maureen through the discomfort of a biopsy. I'm very certain that this is the unfortunate circumstance, as I have seen this before. Maureen and your family have a very difficult road ahead in the coming months."

Michael and Sharon inquired if there was anything that could possibly be done.

The doctor responded, "I understand your pain. I can see it clearly in your faces. I'm sorry to inform you that there's nothing that can be done, except, eventually, Maureen's doctor will prescribe morphine for the pain. A registered nurse will have to administer the morphine. I must advise you, that it will be a difficult and grueling death. I'll contact Maureen's doctor in Buffalo and assist him in any manner I can. Please convey to your mother that I think she has done a fabulous job in caring for Maureen. Also, advise her that the prognosis would be no different if Maureen were brought to my attention earlier. There is, unfortunately, nothing we can do."

Then the inevitable question was asked. "How long does Maureen have to live, Doctor?"

The doctor replied, "I know these are the most trying of circumstances, and my heart bleeds for your mother, knowing she has two children with DEB. In my estimation, your sister Maureen has approximately six months to live."

Michael and Sharon were in a state of shock. This experience for them was certainly reminiscent of the experience with their father. They worried not only for themselves, but especially for Maureen, and particularly for their mother. The siblings made a quick decision not to mention this information to Maureen on the trip home. They decided it would be more appropriate to consult with the entire family so Maureen would be surrounded with love and support. They agreed they would tell Maureen that the doctor would be in touch with her doctor in Buffalo.

The sixty-mile drive from Rochester seemed like a six-hundred mile drive. Michael and Sharon were worried about the impact this would have on their mother, not only emotionally, but physically. They tried desperately to pass the time, engaging Maureen in some cheerful conversation to calm her nerves from this experience.

As Michael, Sharon, and Maureen arrived home, Irene was once again waiting at the front door. As was the case with their father, Irene could read the pain in Michael and Sharon's faces. Despite their best efforts to conceal their pain for Maureen's sake, Irene knew intuitively that the news would not be good.

Irene had a special meal prepared for Maureen, already placed on the kitchen table. After Maureen was carried to the kitchen table and began to feed herself, Irene and her children retreated to the living room. The entire experience in Rochester was communicated from beginning to end, as Irene insisted it be done for her sake. She sat on the sofa and said, "Oh, my Lord. My poor darling doesn't deserve this." Irene didn't even cry, stating that she felt as though she had already expended a lifetime of tears. Time would naturally prove differently, but her statement speaks volumes of her total exasperation and incomprehensible sorrow.

Other family members were notified. There was also a conversation with Maureen's doctor. It was decided, between Irene and the doctor, that Maureen would not immediately be informed that she was terminally ill. That painful moment would come soon enough. The prognosis meant that Maureen would be expected to pass away in July or August, so her upcoming birthday in February would be her last celebration of a birthday with her family.

Maureen was eventually told the news in as delicate a fashion as possible while surrounded by her loving family. Maureen implored all of her family and Christian friends to pray for a miracle. Those were her last words to her dying father, "Please, Daddy, when you get to heaven, please ask Jesus to send a miracle."

While visiting one day with Michael at the kitchen table, Maureen confided in him, that if she was going to die, she would first love to see the ocean. "Michael, I've only seen the ocean on television. I saw this one program about a place called Atlantic City. Well, it had the grandest hotels and a boardwalk right on the beach filled with countless shops. Oh, how I would love to ride my wheelchair down that boardwalk and just look at and listen to the ocean! Can you imagine that, Michael? A boardwalk directly on the beach of the ocean! I've never stayed in a fancy hotel or eaten in a fancy restaurant. I feel as though I've spent most of my life in this kitchen chair, watching everyone else come and go, sharing about all the places they've traveled to. It's not that I'm complaining, Michael. Everyone has been very good to me and I'm very fortunate. But I'd love to stay in a fancy hotel for once, with plush carpeting and a fancy restaurant; a hotel that's directly on the boardwalk, with an ocean view from my window. Oh, Michael, wouldn't that be so wonderful, so much fun?"

Michael responded to his sister by saying, "You have a birthday coming up very soon. I say we turn your birthday party into a fundraiser, so we can make your dream come true! We can take a short flight to Atlantic City. We can book a room with an ocean view in the fanciest hotel on the boardwalk and we can shop all day long. What do you think, should we try to do this? I'll need your help."

"Oh, Michael, are you serious? Do you really mean this? We would actually fly on an airplane? I've never been on an airplane in my entire life! We would actually see and hear the ocean, stay in a fancy hotel, and eat in fancy restaurants? Do you think Mom will allow this?"

"Buckle your seatbelt and get ready for takeoff!" exclaimed an excited Michael, after seeing the delight on Maureen's face. John also was enthusiastically absorbing the entire conversation, presuming that he would be invited along on the trip. "You let me worry about Mom, Maureen. We'll invite Mom along for the experience. We'll raise enough money for your expenses, John's expenses, your nurse's expenses, and Mom's expenses. How could Mom turn down such an adventure? Other members of the family will be invited on the trip at their own expense. I know others will want to come. I know I'll be there, but we have a lot of work to do if we're going to pull this off. We have to get started right away. You think about it."

Maureen's spirits soared above the clouds! "Oh, Michael, I don't want my last birthday to be a sad occasion. I want my last birthday to be a lot of fun. Everyone that I'm going to invite, I'm going to tell them they have to come to my party dressed as a clown, including myself. I want to be dressed as a clown!

"We'll start the celebration, as usual, with a Mass. And after Communion, I want that song called, 'The Rose' to be sung. You must know that song, Michael. The one that says, 'It's the soul afraid of dying that never learns to live.' It ends by saying, 'Just remember, in the winter, far beneath the winter's snow, lies the seed, that with the sun's love, in the spring, becomes a rose.' Except I want the word 'sun's' printed in the program as 'Son's'. While that song is being sung, I want to take a single, red rose up to the altar as a symbol of placing my life in the hand's of Jesus."

Michael, Maureen and the rest of the family got busy. Once again, with the help of the local media, the guest list grew to be in the hundreds! Irene's friends from the parish and the prayer group all cooked something for a pot-luck dinner to be served in the church hall. Michael had an artistic friend construct and decorate, in a circus theme, a large box for guests to deposit their donations. It was planned as a top-notch affair. Maureen enjoyed all the commotion surrounding the planning of the event. She began counting the days until her grand celebration.

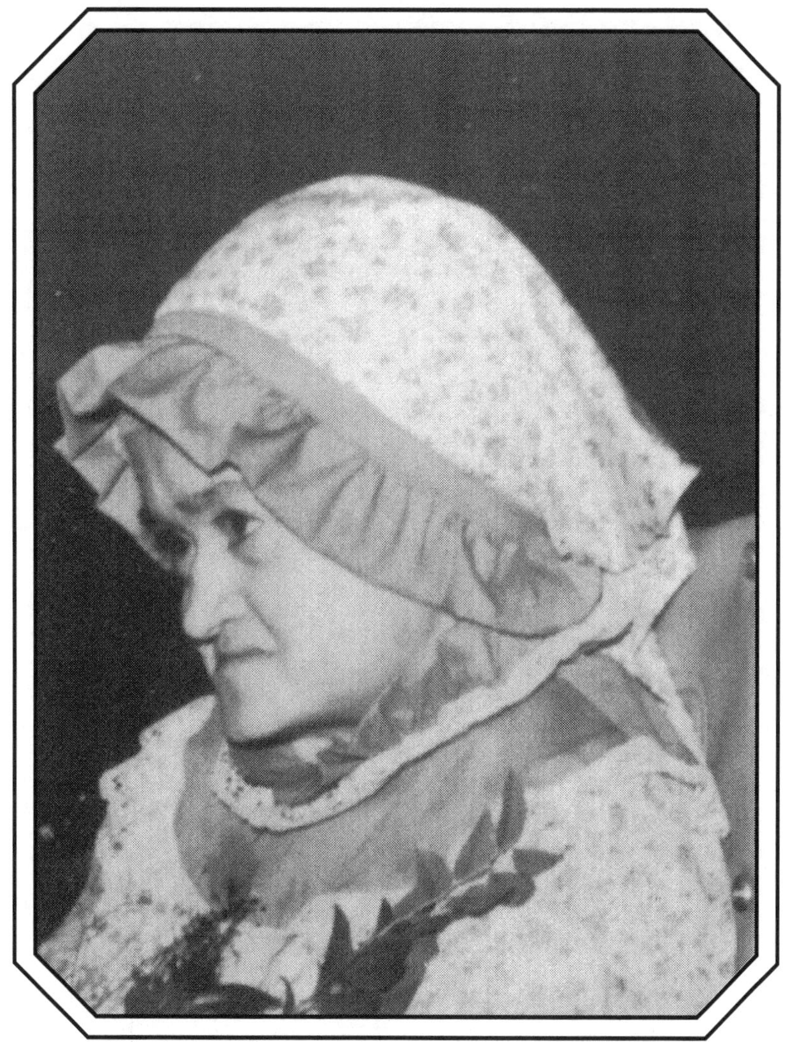

Bearing a single, red rose, Maureen prepares for her 27th and final birthday celebration.

The day finally arrived. Maureen had a special gown sewn for the occasion. She and her brother John had their faces painted as clowns and then, off to the church they went. Michael thought to himself, "This is the most peculiar thing I've ever seen," as he watched the church filling up with people dressed as clowns. Some familiar people were unrecognizable in their costumes. If the pastor was okay with it, well, then anything to put a smile on Maureen's face, even if, on this occasion, it was a painted smile.

The celebrant gave a most moving homily that touched everyone deeply. After communion, a dear friend of Maureen's, with a gifted voice, sang "The Rose." There wasn't a dry eye in the church, as the invited guests watched Maureen lay a single red rose at the foot of the altar, precisely as the lyrics, "It's the soul afraid of dying, that never learns to live," were being sung.

Irene's face was radiant with pride. She reflected back on the day Maureen was born and Dick had presented her with the gold necklace containing a single, red rose. Irene was wearing that necklace. It seemed as though it were just yesterday that Maureen was born. How she wished she could go up and just hug and squeeze her lovely innocent, daughter. That was a pleasure Irene had been denied every day of Maureen's twenty-seven years.

The tempo changed at the venue. Maureen proudly sat at the head table and felt almost as if she were celebrating her wedding! There was plenty of delicious food, music, singing, and dancing. Maureen was enjoying herself fully, almost forgetting that this was her last birthday celebration. However, that realization never escaped Irene's mind. Once again, local media covered the event.

After Maureen returned home, she and Michael began opening the cards in the decorative box. Michael would read the inscribed sentiments and Maureen would count the money. Additional cards and donations followed, and Maureen would wait daily for the arrival of the mail.

Michael finally announced, "Well, we have successfully reached our goal! We're on our way to Atlantic City in early spring for three full days. I've booked your room in a gorgeous hotel on the boardwalk, I mean, as soon as you walk out the door of the hotel, you'll be on the boardwalk. You'll see and hear the ocean and it's waves pounding the sand on the beach. You'll smell the salt from the ocean in the air. Your room has a full view of the ocean and the boardwalk. Maureen, thanks be to God, your dream has come true! We'll travel in April and I believe the rest of the family is joining you at their own expense. It will be the grandest time!" Michael could hardly contain himself when he witnessed the expression of sheer delight cross Maureen's face.

"Oh, Michael, I love you so much! Thank you for doing all of this!"

Michael simply responded, "Hey, don't thank me, thank the Lord. He made it all possible when others thought it would be impossible."

As the plane taxied down the runway, Maureen was grinning ear to ear. She became a little nervous when the engines roared and the plane lifted off the ground. All the family members were capturing the delightful expressions on Maureen's face, that they would remember forever. It seemed that in no time at all the plane landed, and Maureen was being shuttled to her hotel and escorted to her room, with her family sharing in her excitement.

"Oh, this room is so gorgeous! Quick, take me to my window, I want to see the ocean! Oh, look at that!" exclaimed an elated Maureen. "The ocean! It looks magnificent! You can't even see the other side of the ocean, it's so big! Well, what are we waiting for? Let's go down on the boardwalk!"

Everyone joined Maureen on the boardwalk. Her enthusiasm could not be contained and was quite contagious. One of the first shops Maureen spotted was a specialty hat store for women. She went in and slowly shopped around with Stephen's wife. "I've never seen so many beautiful hats in one place before in my entire life!" she exclaimed. Maureen rolled out of that shop wearing a brand new, wide brimmed bonnet that she'd fallen in love with. She wore that bonnet everywhere she went for the rest of the trip.

It soon came time for dinner. Maureen could hardly wait to experience the ambiance of an elegant restaurant with the rest of the family. She proudly wore her new bonnet. Some special arrangements had to be made for John and Maureen in terms of the preparation of their food.

The restaurant was more than accommodating. Everyone enjoyed a savory meal.

When it came time to request the check, the waiter informed the O'Briens that their bill was taken care of, compliments of the famous billiard player, Willie Mosconi. Mr. Mosconi made his way over to the O'Brien table and introduced himself to Maureen. He leaned over, ducking beneath the broadly rimmed bonnet, and kissed Maureen on the cheek, saying to her, "You look as beautiful as a princess!" Maureen blushed. No one outside the family had ever spoken such words to her. Rather, Maureen had grown accustomed to people gawking at her, which, given her sensitive nature, always made her feel deeply hurt.

These words were like a symphony to Maureen's ears! She turned to her mother and said, "You know, Mom, that man made me feel so beautiful. Now I finally know what it's like to get all dressed up and go to the prom with a date! I think it was the bonnet that made all the difference."

Irene's heart was torn in two; she ached for her daughter, realizing the many forms of suffering she had endured her entire life, yet at the same time, she wanted to kiss Willie Mosconi's feet for the memorable experience he had created for her daughter. Irene would never forget that moment and would always remember Maureen's sweet words.

The trip was over all too soon, but Maureen came home with a storehouse of experiences to share with her friends.

On the top of the list was her "date" with Willie Mosconi. Maureen also enjoyed showing off her new bonnet and often wore it, even in the house.

As time passed, Irene noticed that the tumors were growing in size and rapidly multiplying in number. It was not very long before the tumors made it challenging for Maureen to get comfortable sitting in a chair or reclining on her bed. Irene also noticed that Maureen's appetite was rapidly decreasing and she was becoming gaunt in her appearance. The family noticed all these signs also, and made frequent trips to the house to check on her and support their mother. Friends of the family were remarkably helpful.

John was having a very difficult time with the entire process of Maureen's dying. On a couple of occasions, John was less than kind to Maureen. A shallow person may have accused John of being insensitive, but anyone who truly understood John, realized that he was suffering over the impending death of his sister. Maureen had been his partner for most of his life. The kitchen table would seem so empty to John without Maureen in her chair, just as it had seemed so empty when John lost his father. Additionally, one could not help but wonder if John was thinking that he was previewing his own agonizing death, one that would befall him in the near future. Certainly, they had their arguments like any siblings do, but there was an inseparable bond between the two that only an insider could truly appreciate.

Michael caught a glimpse of this bond in action one afternoon while visiting at the house. John was seated next to Maureen at the kitchen table. She had her forehead placed on the rim of a bowl that was placed on the table because she was so nauseous. Michael was seated in the family room reading the paper, when he heard Maureen coughing and vomiting, so he looked out into the kitchen to ascertain whether she needed any assistance. Michael saw John extend his clubbed hand over toward Maureen. She reached out and rested her hand on John's hand. Michael was aware that his brother and sister understood each other better than anyone else in the world. No one could question their deep bond of love as symbolized by the embracing of their hands. John and Maureen were wounded healers to each other.

As the days and weeks passed, Maureen became more uncomfortable, lost her appetite completely, and was more gaunt than ever. Rarely did Maureen have the strength to sit up in a chair. Instead, a little "nest" was made for Maureen to recline in on one of the love seats in the living room. Maureen was in agony. Morphine was being administered. She would be gingerly carried up to her bed in the evening.

Michael made his daily stop at the house to check on Maureen. As he pulled in the driveway, the garage door was open with Irene's gray Toyota parked inside. It was obvious that Irene had returned from her daily Mass and forgot to close the garage door. Michael decided to enter the house through the garage door instead of the front door. The front door would have led directly to the stairwell in the center of the house. Instead, he entered the family room and then passed through the kitchen and dining room to the stairwell.

As Michael stood at the bottom of the stairs, he witnessed his mother ascending the stairs on her knees. Unaware of Michael's presence, at each stair, Irene would bless herself and whisper, "Oh, my dear Lord, have mercy on me and give me strength. Let your power be made perfect in my weakness." Then she would ascend another stair, bless herself, and repeat the same prayers with even greater fervor. When Irene reached the top stair, she used the railing to pull herself up from her knees. Then she walked into John and Maureen's room as radiant as a sunny day in July, proclaiming, "Well, how are we doing today, my darlings? Did we sleep well?"

Tears welled up in Michael's eyes. He was astonished at the depth of his mother's faith, and her utter reliance on the Lord to strengthen her to do the Father's will pertaining to the delicate care of her dying daughter. He will never forget that sight of his mother. It is indelibly engraved in his mind and soul. Michael never respected and appreciated his mother more than he did in that private, precious moment.

Family members were over at the house celebrating a sibling's birthday. Maureen had been "nested" in her love seat and was receiving morphine that was beginning to do little for her agony. As the family was starting to leave, Maureen was carefully carried to her bed. It seemed as though little was left of her except for those tumors.

As Michael was preparing to leave, Maureen sent someone to retrieve him. He hastened up the stairs to see what she wanted. Maureen asked, "Michael, can you sleep on the floor next to me tonight?" Without hesitation, he asserted he would be delighted to spend the night.

Michael called his employer to be excused from work until further notice. He went to the basement and retrieved a sleeping bag which he placed between the beds. Michael said, "I feel like I'm camping! I hope there are no other wild animals in this room besides the two of you!" He heard a faint chuckle come from Maureen's direction and he felt fulfilled that he could do something for his sister.

From that moment forward, at Maureen's request, Michael never left his sister's side. It was not long before Maureen ended up spending the nights, as well as the days, in her love seat "nest", with Michael on the floor beside her. One morning, Maureen, in a very frail whisper, requested that her mother do her dressings immediately.

Irene responded, "You want your dressings done now, Sweetheart? Sure, I can do your dressings now."

Two of Irene's friends, who were members of the prayer group, happened to stop at the house. Maureen weighed next to nothing, so Irene was able to carry her up the stairs with no effort and place her gingerly on her bed to do her dressings. John was already awake in his own bed. Michael and the two friends followed Irene into Maureen's bedroom. Maureen kept her eyes closed the entire time.

As Irene carefully unwrapped all of Maureen's bandages, Michael looked at Maureen's naked body with all those tumors and how disfigured her body appeared. All he could think of was the Passion of Christ and how badly His body was beaten. With Irene, John, Michael, and the two friends in the room as witnesses, Maureen suddenly opened her eyes, stretched her neck to look above and behind her, and then nodded her head "yes." Sensing a holy presence in the room, the two prayer group friends dropped to their knees. Maureen then repeated the same action another time. Now, Michael and Irene were on their knees. For a third and final time, Maureen opened her eyes, looked up and behind her, and nodded "yes." Then Maureen very peacefully drew her last breath.

Irene picked up the naked, disfigured body of her baby and started to weep. She sat down on the only chair in the room, embracing Maureen tightly in her arms. Crying hysterically, she wept, "Oh my darling! Since the day you were born, over twenty-seven years ago, I have wanted to squeeze you, to hug you, and to smother you with my kisses.

I shall not be denied any longer! I love you so dearly, my sweetheart! When you asked me about the prom, I wanted to hug you so tightly at that moment, and console you, but I couldn't. You would have been the Prom Queen! Oh, my dear Lord, how I love my little darling!"

Irene embraced Maureen firmly while kissing her entire body. Irene made a special point of kissing each and every tumor, repeating, "Oh my darling, I can finally hug and kiss you and smother you with my love!"

Blood streamed from Maureen's disfigured body, saturating Irene's clothes, and then dripping onto the carpeted floor. Irene paid no attention. She was compensating for the twenty-seven years she had to deny her maternal instincts. It was like a dam had burst and was flooding the room with the sorrow she had endured for so long. The two women from the prayer group were on the floor weeping hysterically at the sight of Irene, as they listened to her mournful words. The friends were so distraught for Irene that they were literally pulling pieces of the shagged carpeting from the floor. John was crying out his sister's name repeatedly, "Maureen! Maureen! Oh, Maureen! How I am going to survive without you?" It was a gut-wrenching scene.

Michael was fixated on the scene of his mournful mother, squeezing and hugging Maureen with blood flowing in every direction. *The Pieta! I am witnessing a living Pieta!*

Naturally, the church was filled to capacity for Maureen's funeral, with people in the balcony and standing in the aisles; several priests concelebrated the Mass. After the distribution of Communion, Maureen's friend sang "The Rose." "Just remember, in the winter, far beneath the bitter snow, lies the seed, that with the Son's love, in the spring, becomes a rose." The friend then placed a single red rose on top of Maureen's casket. Irene grasped onto the rose necklace presented by Dick on the occasion of Maureen's birth and simply wept.

Maureen's wide brimmed bonnet, the one that made her feel so beautiful, had been placed on her casket along with the rose, as it was wheeled to the back of the church. There was not a dry eye in the church, as guests witnessed Irene O'Brien, a widow, about to bury her second child.

The funeral procession proceeded on Route 90 and eventually accessed Route 96A. At that blinking signal light, the procession made a right hand turn onto Main Street in the tiny village of Ovid, New York. When the procession came to Gilbert Road, it made a right hand turn and entered the third driveway of Holy Cross Cemetery and proceeded to just about the end of the road. There, on the left side, was a fresh grave for Maureen Clare O'Brien. The widow, Irene Marie Corcoran O'Brien, buried her second child, in the same place she used to dream of her future when she was just a little girl.

It was summer, August as a matter of fact. There were no tiger lilies, no butterflies, no fireflies, no cherries left on the trees, but the farmers' fields were rich with grain and corn ready to be harvested.

Chapter Eleven

SHE PONDERED THESE THINGS IN HER HEART

Be still and know that I am God (Psalm 46:10).

Does history repeat itself? Can lightning strike the same place more than once? Any member of the O'Brien clan would answer that question affirmatively without hesitation. It had been almost eight years since John's younger sister Maureen passed away from squamous cell carcinoma as a complication of her DEB. John was now thirty-nine years old and Irene seventy-one years old.

John acclimated quite well to life without his companion, Maureen. His personality was more independent than Maureen's fragile, sensitive personality. That is not to suggest that John did not miss his sister. He spoke of her quite often. In fact, John frequently requested Michael to, "Please pray that I have a peaceful death like Maureen did." She lived on in John's heart and in his memories. It was as though he were a bird that learned to fly with one wing.

It is certainly true that an aging Irene never let a day pass without thinking of Maureen. Tennyson's words, "If I had a flower for every time I thought of you, I could walk through my garden forever," would readily apply to Irene. She also included Dick and Ricky in her daily thoughts.

John was almost forty years old and the disease had taken its toll on his deformed body. Because of Irene's age, she relied more heavily on the assistance of aides and nurses in the ever-increasing, complex care of John. At the time, John was believed to be the oldest living survivor afflicted with the dreadful disease. When no nurses were available, Irene would adeptly do his dressings. This was no easy task for a woman over seventy years old, but no one ever heard a complaint issue forth from Irene's mouth. The skilled nursing care would often comment to her, "I can't believe you've done this every day for the past thirty-nine years!"

One particular morning, the nurse called Irene into John's bedroom as John's dressings were being done. The nurse pointed to several white spots on John's raw back, inquiring of Irene what these spots might be. Irene knew all too well that those spots were indicative of impending serious problems. She sighed and lifted her hands to the Lord. Then, she spoke compassionately to John, "We're going to need to have the doctor take a look at this, John." John was astute enough to understand the fate of the future that awaited him in the months to come. Could Irene possibly endure the indescribable pain of a mother's heart as she would watch another of her beloved children become the innocent victim of an agonizing death? After all, had John not suffered enough throughout his life?

John beseeched his brother Michael to provide a "Dream Come True Trip" for him, as he had so successfully done for his sister Maureen. However, John had more extravagant ideas mulling in his head. He implored Michael, "Please get me to Las Vegas! I've always wanted to play a slot machine. The Lord must surely understand I could use some good luck!"

Michael was more than willing to comply with John's request, not merely for John's sake, but particularly for the sake of his mother. Michael appreciated the fact that if Irene saw John occupied and happy, his mother's burden would be somewhat lifted. Michael realized he was embarking on an enormous task, so he solicited the assistance of two of his dearest friends, Peg and Katie; they felt honored to assist.

When the doctor learned of John's desire to travel to Las Vegas, he placed a call to Michael. He told him, "If you're going to do this, you need to do it sooner than later."

Michael understood that the doctor was suggesting that John's prognosis was not a favorable one. He inquired of the doctor how much time he would have to plan and execute the trip. The doctor replied, "Make the trip no later than September."

Being that John just recently celebrated his thirty-ninth birthday on the first day of July, he realized he would need to immediately plan how to make John's ambitious dream a reality for him. The clock was ticking and Michael could hear the hands of the clock as each hour passed.

The concept emerged that Michael would sponsor a pre-fortieth birthday party for his brother John. He contacted Bishop Head and requested that John's pre-fortieth party begin with a Mass celebrated in the Cathedral; the Bishop was most empathetic and willing to assist. The Bishop then gave Michael the dates of his availability. Next, Michael went to Buffalo's largest venue for banquet dining that was conveniently located near the Cathedral. The venue, fortunately, was open the same evening the Bishop was available to celebrate Mass.

The idea was presented to John by Michael, Peg, and Kate; he was thrilled and very grateful. John wanted the grandest birthday party he ever celebrated! He specifically requested that he wanted a head table to sit at with his family. John enthusiastically added that he wanted a few, select friends to share a few words with a microphone. In John's terminology, "This will be the closest thing to a wedding that I'll ever have! Michael, you're my best man!" John wasted no time calling his friends to spread the word about his impending party.

Seeing John happy, and assisting in the planning of his extravaganza, did indeed somewhat lighten Irene's heart. She was happy that John had something to look forward to and something positive to occupy his mind, at least for the moment. She understood painfully well what was waiting in the wings for her fifth child.

A friend inquired of Irene, "Do you think John will be able to endure traveling that long distance, not to mention tolerating the desert heat?"

Irene responded, "Look, if John dies fulfilling a dream, then praise the Lord!"

Michael called some prayer group friends and requested they make a special, banner-style altar cloth that would read "A Heroic Celebration of Life" and include some shamrocks. This was to become the theme of the evening. The friends happily complied and created a beautiful altar cloth; Irene was deeply impressed.

Michael called all the local media, and being familiar with John, they were more than happy to assist in promoting the event. A printer called to donate the admission tickets that were to be sold as a fundraiser for the formal dinner following the celebration of Mass. The tickets would read, "A Heroic Celebration of Life." An airline that flies non-stop to Las Vegas called Michael and donated four, first-class seats. The banquet hall called Michael and informed him that the manager was waiving the rental fee and would only charge for food. When Michael called the newest luxury, high-rise in Las Vegas to inquire about a room, the hotel donated the Penthouse Suite! The Lord was opening all sorts of doors and was richly blessing John.

Tickets were selling like hotcakes! John was ecstatic and appreciative of the combined efforts of Michael and his friends. John made a list of the select few that he wanted to speak that evening during dinner and began giving them a call.

What John did not know, was that Michael had called Buffalo's superstar, four-time AFC Championship Quarterback, Jim Kelly, to inquire if he could possibly appear as a surprise speaker. Jim Kelly was John's personal hero. John never missed a Bill's game on television. He cheered Jim Kelly on to victory, time and time again. "Oh, if I could only hold and throw a football like Jim Kelly!" John used to say repeatedly.

Jim Kelly was scheduled to be out of town the weekend of the extravaganza. However, Jim was thoughtful enough to record a personal, ten minute videotape addressing John as "his personal hero." The tape was mailed to Michael and was kept and secured as "top secret" from everyone. Maureen wanted clowns; John was going to get Jim Kelly.

Just as Maureen had selected "The Rose" to be played after Communion at her Mass, John had also selected a song. His favorite song, recorded by Whitney Houston, was "Give Me One Moment In Time." Michael had a friend who was an extremely gifted vocalist who happily agreed to perform the song at the Cathedral.

The evening finally arrived. John made sure he and his family were the first to arrive at the Cathedral and sit in the front row. It was not long before the Cathedral was filled. Irene processed everything in complete awe. Finally, Bishop Head began the Mass. Bishop Head spoke profound words to John and Irene that encouraged them both, while amazing all those in attendance. While Communion was being distributed, John eagerly watched the faces of his guests as they came forward.

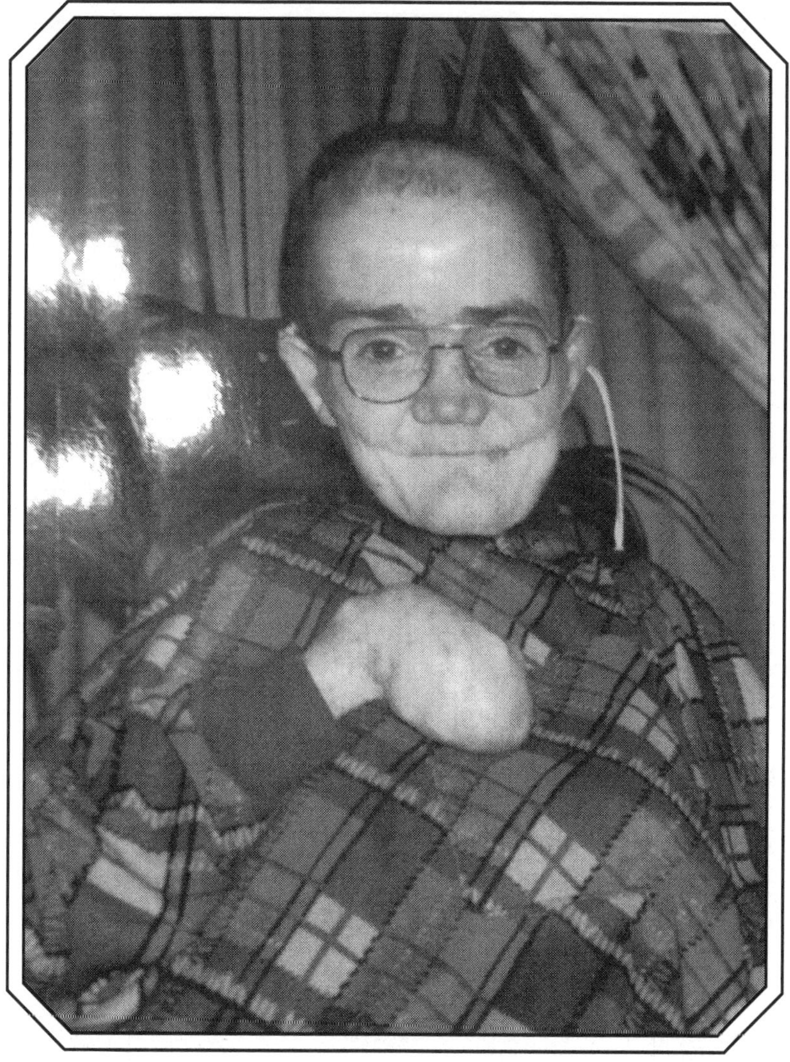

John dresses for his 39th and final birthday celebration.

After the distribution of Communion, there was silent meditation. Then the organ played, and an angelic voice could be heard from the choir loft. "I broke my heart, fought every gain. To taste the sweet, I faced the pain. I rise and fall, yet through it all, this much remains; I want one moment in time, when I'm more than I thought I could be, when all of my dreams are a heartbeat away, and the answers are all up to me. Give me one moment in time, when I'm racing with destiny, then, in that one moment in time, I will feel, I will feel eternity." John's friends had gathered in prayer to grant John his one moment in time after thirty-nine years of sheer agony.

When the celebration of Mass was complete, Bishop Head was generous enough to come down from the altar and greet all of the O'Briens. Irene pulled the Bishop to herself in a warm embrace, thanking him immensely. The Bishop informed John that he would stop by the dinner venue but would be unable to remain for dinner. John had only gratitude for all the Bishop had done for him, recounting the previous home Mass, as well as all the visits to the hospital.

Bishop Head poses with John and Irene.

Finally, John was escorted to the dinner venue. He was overwhelmed when he first caught a glimpse of the elegance of the banquet hall. He was placed at the center of the head table surrounded by his family, including several nieces and nephews who faithfully demonstrated their devotion to John over the years. Michael's friend Peg orchestrated the evening from the podium with such elegance and dignity that some in the crowd wondered if the O'Briens had hired a public speaker. Peg introduced those whom John had chosen to speak on his behalf.

Then, after the last speaker completed his remarks, Peg called the audience's attention to a big screen monitor provided by the venue. Michael inserted the tape from Jim Kelly. The crowd was astonished! John wept as he listened attentively to the words of Jim Kelly; his heart filling with gratitude. At the conclusion of Jim Kelly's remarks, the crowd jumped to their feet in a thunderous standing ovation. Irene also stood, looked over at her son who was wiping tears of joy from his face, and with her Irish eyes smiling, gave John a kiss on the cheek.

As per the doctor's directive, the plans to travel to Las Vegas were finalized for mid-September. John loved the music of Wayne Newton. Upon learning that Wayne Newton was playing in Las Vegas, John implored that attendance at one of his concerts be included in the agenda. John's doctor also highly recommended that he see a show by the masters of illusion, Siegfried and Roy. Michael booked reservations for four at each of the venues, at John's insistence. It was determined that Michael, and two nurses, would accompany John on his excursion to Las Vegas. Irene was comfortable with those arrangements.

John had experienced flying two times in his life. The first was the flight to Atlantic City with his sister Maureen. John's second flight was aboard a private, corporate jet to view the opening of the play in Cleveland. However, this would be John's longest flight and he was thrilled! Anticipation of the Vegas excursion occupied John's mind much of the day, pushing the anxiety of his impending death to the corners of his mind. Seeing John so happy filled Irene's heart with delight.

An excited John flies off to Las Vegas.

John landed in Las Vegas and was shuttled to his hotel; everything had exceeded his wildest expectations. As John was wheeled into his Penthouse Suite from a private elevator, he broke out in hysterics as he witnessed the awe that overcame everyone's faces! John would occupy the master bedroom, and the nurses would occupy the two queen beds provided by the second bedroom. Michael booked a separate room in a cheaper hotel. John enjoyed a beautiful view of the Las Vegas strip from his suite and was amazed at all the dazzling lights once evening fell. Irene was soothed each time she spoke with John on the telephone because his enthusiasm wasn't waning.

In the morning, Michael went to the stage door of the venue that was hosting Wayne Newton. He explained the purpose of the trip to Vegas to the stagehand and informed him that his brother would be in the audience that evening. Michael left copies of media reports with the stagehand to share with Mr. Newton.

Michael had reserved a booth close to center stage. As the foursome arrived for the concert, John was excited about being so close to the stage. He became even more excited when the house lights dimmed, the orchestra began to play, and Wayne Newton made a splashy entrance onto the stage. Many of the songs were familiar to John, and if his smile was a measure of his elation, he was enjoying the show more than anyone else in the theater.

Then suddenly, about halfway through the show, Mr. Newton unexpectedly stopped and inquired where John O'Brien was seated. John's jaw dropped as a stage light searched the audience until it fell upon him. Mr. Newton came to the edge of the stage and engaged John in a brief conversation. Then, Mr. Newton dedicated a medley of appropriate songs to John. Tears streamed down John's face as well as the faces of the nurses; they were all in a state of shock. Michael had revealed his secret meeting with the stagehand to no one. Irene slept peacefully that night after listening to John's enthusiastic recount of the events at the concert.

John had a surprise for Michael too. That evening, following the show, the four went to dinner; John made the reservations. Everyone talked and laughed about how amazing the show was. Then, after the main course was finished, the waitress came out with candles aglow on a birthday cake. It was Michael's birthday, and in appreciation for all he had done for John, John surprised his brother while the restaurant joined the waitress in singing "Happy Birthday." John shared some sentimental words in a toast to his brother. Now, tears were rolling down Michael's cheeks.

Then John asked his brother a question, "Michael, will you promise me that you'll be by my side when it comes time for me to die?"

Michael candidly replied, "John, I promise I will do my best to be at your side when you die."

"Not good enough," retorted John. "I need you to promise that you'll, in fact, be at my side when I die. The Lord chose you to be by Ricky, Dad, and Maureen when they died. I know He has chosen you to be with me also." The nurses were stunned and remained silent as they awaited Michael's reply.

Michael felt the gentle voice of the Holy Spirit in the deepest recesses of his heart, affirming John's words. He looked directly into John's eyes and responded, "Well, if the Lord has chosen me as you say, then I'll be at your side when you die, John." John was at peace with that response.

The next evening was the Siegfried and Roy show. John had never seen an illusionist in his entire life, so he didn't know quite what to expect. He just knew that his doctor advised him that he must not miss the show.

While they were seated and awaiting the specially constructed auditorium to fill, a Maitre d' approached the table and inquired of Michael, "Sir, how did you pay for this booth?"

Michael quickly replied, "With my credit card. Why are you asking? Is there a problem?"

"No sir," the Maitre d' responded. "Mr. Siegfried would like to pay for this booth. He would like for you to be his guests. If you hand me your credit card, I will take care of the transaction."

The nurses were more astonished than John, who was in hysterics once again. Everyone was pleased with how perfectly the trip was unfolding, but no one was more pleased than Irene, waiting at home.

The trip seemed to pass too quickly for John. However, his heart was filled with deep appreciation, and his mind was bursting with exciting memories to share with his mother and friends in the weeks to come.

Those weeks were brutally cruel to John. By early November, he was gaunt and required morphine, which was administered by a nurse with a dropper directly into John's mouth. John looked like a baby bird opening its mouth wide, waiting for its mother to feed it, each time he needed a dose of the morphine.

The Wednesday before Thanksgiving, Michael received a telephone call at work from his mother. Irene was crying with such heartfelt sobs that it was difficult to understand what she was attempting to say. Michael finally deciphered the words, "John is requesting your presence."

Remembering his promise to John, Michael excused himself from work immediately and rushed home. When he entered the house, he found John "nested" in one of the love seats in the living room, in the same fashion that had been done for Maureen. Other family members were already there. Michael announced his presence to John and assured his brother that he was there to stay.

Michael refused to leave his brother's side. He was determined to keep his promise that was sealed in Las Vegas. Thanksgiving Day passed. On Friday, family members encouraged Michael to leave at least long enough to shower and shave. They promised him they would call him if there was the slightest change in John's condition. They prodded Michael saying, "John won't even recognize you if you don't shower and shave." Michael complied, took the fastest shower of his life and promptly returned to John.

It was now Saturday. Most of the family was at the house in support of John and their mother. John was carried to his bedroom early Saturday evening. The vigil continued in John's bedroom, everyone was astonished that he was still alive. Stephen spoke soothing words to John. Cassie comforted him. Michael looked at his brother. *My Lord, he looks like a vacuum-sealed skeleton.* Irene finally went to bed at 11:00 p.m. requesting to be awakened if there were any change.

At 11:30, in an extremely frail whisper, John called for his brother Michael. Michael knelt down next to John's side and took a firm hold of his brother's clubbed hand. He leaned over and spoke loudly into John's ear, stating simply, "I'm here as I promised I would be!" He felt John's hand move in his grasp. *Michael, promise me you'll be with me when I die. That is not good enough of an answer. Promise you will be with me when I die. The Lord has chosen you. You were there for Ricky, Dad, and Maureen. The Lord has chosen you. Promise you'll be with me when I die. The Lord has chosen you. The Lord has chosen you. The Lord has chosen you.*

Patrick summoned his mother. Irene walked into the room and kissed John on the forehead and then blessed him. Irene finally spoke, "It's time John. It's time to meet Jesus. Go, and visit Ricky, your Dad, and Maureen." Family members in the room were sobbing, but they cheered John on to cross the finish line and claim his prize. Finally, John took his last breath.

The doctor and undertaker were called, and arrived in a matter of minutes. Irene turned to Patrick, who had been such a faithful servant to John over the years and directed, "Patrick, don't let them come up here and take John. Would you please carry your brother out of the house for the last time?" Patrick swooped up his brother into his broad arms and carried John through the front door for the last time, as the family gave John a thunderous ovation.

The church was filled to capacity, with people standing in the aisles and in the back for the funeral. All three local television networks had their cameras and light stands assembled. Nearly twenty priests concelebrated the Mass, with the pastor being the principal celebrant and homilist. The pastor commented what a miracle it was, as evidenced by the crowd in the church and the presence of the media, that John was able to transform so many lives from the confines of his kitchen chair.

The pastor then read a message that John had dictated for his brother Michael. "Michael, you are the gift of joy, the educator, the planner. You gave me some of the most memorable days of my life by granting my wishes that I could never have dreamed up. You moved heaven and earth for me, and knowing your relationship with the Lord, I know you moved heaven. You also prepared me for the hardest journey, going home, by soothing my fears and promising me that I would not be alone. When wonderful things start happening to you, Michael, give credit where credit is due. For you see, I now have the connections to move heaven and earth. Michael, you gave me one moment in time, many times over." Irene held Michael's hand firmly, leaning over to kiss him on the cheek, whispering a heartfelt thank you into his ear.

The pastor also recounted how John used to watch Stephen play football in the backyard. John commented that he wished he could play football, but Stephen told him that he would never be able to play. John replied that if he could play football that day, he would be willing to die the next. The pastor concluded, "John's heaven was that which we took for granted every day."

John's brothers carried his casket to the back of the church upon their shoulders, as the vocalist was concluding the song, "Give me one moment in time, I will be, I will be free!"

Yes, the funeral procession followed Route 90 until it eventually reached Route 96A. At the single, blinking light the procession made a right turn onto Main Street in the village of Ovid. When the procession reached Gilbert Road, it turned right and entered the third driveway of Holy Cross Cemetery. There, almost at the end of the drive, on the left hand side, was a fresh grave awaiting the burial of John

Vincent O'Brien, who had survived DEB for nearly forty years.

Michael's eyes were fixed on his mother the entire duration of the graveside service. He didn't hear the words of the prayers; he just stared at his mother the entire time. Irene's face was without emotion; she looked stunned. Here was this woman, seventy-one years old, who was virtually sitting on her husband's grave, a widow for nearly twenty years, and she was burying her third child! Michael sobbed as he wondered what she could possibly be thinking.

Who can sustain such sorrow? Was she remembering the innocent days of her youth? The days she walked Gilbert Road to school, passing this cemetery, dreaming of the day when she would be happily married and have a large, healthy family? What was she possibly experiencing in her heart as she was burying her third child? Michael could only think of the Scripture verse, "But Mary treasured all these things, pondering them in her heart" (Luke 2:9).

Michael drove back to Buffalo with his dear friends, Peg and Kate. In an attempt to console Michael, they prayed for a sign from the Lord that John was enjoying heaven with his brother Ricky and sister Maureen. As the car approached the Seneca Army Depot, three albino deer stood in the corner of the fence, facing the road. As the car approached, the deer kicked up their heels and playfully ran off into the woods!

Chapter Twelve

ABSOLUTELY NOTHING CONTRADICTS GOD'S LOVE FOR US

Michael arrived early to his mother's house, assuring additional travel time to Stephen's house, due to the slow-paced traffic resulting from the snowstorms engulfing the area. Now, Michael was frantically pacing the floor of his mother's family room, threatening to wear a hole in the carpet with his endless circular paths. He was impatiently awaiting the arrival of his siblings with a desperation that cannot be expressed with words. Michael understood it could be as long as an hour before their arrival because his siblings lived well south of Buffalo.

It was Sunday, January 30, 1994. It was not any ordinary Sunday, it was Superbowl Sunday. The entire city of Buffalo, in fact, all of Western New York was psyched-up to watch the Buffalo Bills fourth consecutive attempt to win a Superbowl. Excitement permeated the air as the town was convinced of an ultimate win against the Dallas Cowboys at the Georgia Dome. The O'Briens were enthusiastically awaiting an unprecedented performance by their hero, Jim Kelly, who had been so kind to their brother John. A family celebration was planned at Stephen's house to watch the game. Michael had volunteered to drive his mother through the drifting, January snow, in what is referred to as the "snow belt" area, south of the city.

Michael had just spoken with his mother last evening, to make arrangements for pick-up times and what foods to bring for the Superbowl party. Inadvertently, he had awakened his mother who had already retired for the evening. She laughed as she assured him it was no problem that he had awakened her. Irene had begun to retire earlier since her bout with colon cancer six months previous, which required surgery and chemotherapy. Michael and Irene briefly discussed the arrangements for the next morning, each expressing concerns about the weather forecast.

After speaking with Michael, while listening to the dreadful, howling wind outside her bedroom window Irene was brought back to that blustery morning in January 1934. She recalled the infamous walk down the entire stretch of Gilbert Road to the Seneca County School in one of the worst snowstorms of her lifetime. She pondered how life was but a fleeting moment in time. She was amazed at the detail with which she could remember that morning, recalling with fondness the warm breakfast her loving mother had prepared. She was even able to envision herself dashing back into the house to retrieve her math book and homework from the kitchen table. Most of all, Irene reminisced about how deeply she had to reach inside herself to uncover the promise of brighter days yet to come, and the assurance this was just a passing storm. It suddenly seemed to Irene that she was reliving that very day. *Today is January 30th. Thank God this trying month is almost over. Summer's glory draws nigh! Yes, Summer's glory draws nigh!* She could hear her mother's firm, warm, raspy voice calling her name; a sound that always comforted her. *When you hear your mothers voice, come home immediately.* Finally, completely exhausted, Irene fell into a peaceful slumber.

Realizing that it would be some time before his siblings arrived, a nervous Michael, who was making himself dizzy pacing relentlessly in circles, finally reclined into his favorite chair. Michael's mind began to wander. For some reason, he began remembering his trip to Alaska with his mother.

Michael had been planning his trip to Alaska for nearly a year. The summers of his childhood spent at his grandparents' cottage on the shores of Seneca Lake, had bestowed upon him a gift of tremendous love for nature and the outdoors. Michael was an avid camper who loved the Adirondacks in upstate New York, as well as Algonquin Provincial Park in the northern parts of Canada, but Alaska had always remained his dream trip.

One particular evening, Michael was zealously sharing with his mother every detail of the itinerary for his trip as they were seated at the homestead's kitchen table. Michael described with a contagious enthusiasm the multiple excursions he would be embarking upon while in Alaska. In the midst of their conversation, Irene shocked Michael as she blurted out, "I've always wanted to go to Alaska!"

Michael had no recollection of his mother ever making that comment on a prior occasion. He immediately interpreted his mother's words as a signal that she needed some respite, some excitement, something to look forward to experiencing. Michael opined that perhaps this was his mother's "Dream Come True Trip." After some careful consideration, he extended an invitation for his mother to join him on his sojourn to Alaska, the "Land of the Midnight Sun." Irene wasted no time in accepting the invitation, like a child who feared the opportunity might vanish before her eyes if she didn't act immediately. The departure date was set for late June when the sun does not set in the northern sections of Alaska.

After an incredibly long journey, the plane landed at the airport in Anchorage, Alaska at 11:30 p.m. After retrieving their luggage and rental vehicle, Michael laughed aloud as he found it necessary to don his sunglasses as they made their way to their reserved hotel rooms in downtown Anchorage. It was 11:45 p.m. and the sun was so brilliant it was blinding. Irene remarked, "This is what it must be like in heaven; eternal light."

Irene thoroughly enjoyed everything about Alaska! She and Michael traveled to Denali Park and flew over the peak of Mount Denali. They traveled further north to Fairbanks and enjoyed an informative river cruise. Irene was in awe as she admired the vast glacier-capped mountain ranges, the grizzly bears, caribou, moose, and Dahl sheep. Irene commented to Michael, "My mother used to call nature, 'God's fingerprints.' I've never appreciated her words as much as I have here in Alaska!"

Irene's favorite part of the trip was unquestionably the boat excursions from the shores of Valdez and Seward. These adventures unveiled the miracles of the marine. Michael and Irene were enthralled to be witnessing humpback whales breaching, observing pods of orcas hunting for their prey of sea lions, viewing countless birds including the bald eagle, and Irene's favorite, the puffins.

However, what Irene enjoyed the most about these marine excursions was the boat's ability to approach some of Alaska's most famous glaciers. These passenger boats were able to go where no cruise ship could approach. She just marveled at the gigantic blue glaciers, calling them "Ice Cathedrals." Visiting Alaska was a spiritual experience for Irene. She quoted from Psalm 8, "When I look at your heavens, the work of your fingers, the moon and the stars, which you have set in place." Irene added, "Well, I guess I'm going to have to include, 'When I look at your glaciers.'"

It was about a four hour drive to their final destination in Alaska, three full days on the Homer Spit. As they continued on their ambitious journey, Michael was contemplating the serene expression on his mother's face. Irene appeared to be so at peace. This prompted Michael to engage his mother in a deeply personal conversation that he will always treasure.

"Mother, many people who've experienced only a fraction of the tragedies that have befallen you, would long ago have turned their backs on God. They would've lost their faith and undoubtedly become bitter. Inevitably, they would have questioned, 'How could any loving God have allowed such suffering and tragedy to occur?' You must admit, you've had more than your share of unbearable suffering; you've prayed for miracle upon miracle, and you've received none. Has God turned a deaf ear to you?" lamented Michael. "How is it that you're so strong in your faith and can carry on with such complete joy?"

"Well, you certainly have shared a mouthful, Michael. I'm definitely not a theologian, but allow me to take my time and try my best to address each of the issues you've raised. This isn't a sermon, it's just a mother speaking with her son. So, do your best not to interrupt your poor mother!

"First of all, let me assure you that I'm not strong. I can be counted among the weakest of the weak! When Saint Paul entreated the Lord to remove the thorn from his side on three separate occasions, the Lord replied, 'My grace is sufficient for you, for My power is made perfect in your weakness' (2 Corinthians 12:9). When people call me 'strong' it's God's power they're witnessing, certainly not mine!

"Our weaknesses are like personally, hand-written invitations from the Lord to rely on His grace which is bountifully available if we seek it. We have the free will to accept or decline the invitation. I waste no time in accepting the invitation throughout each and every day. That's how weak I feel in the face of the daunting tasks He has bestowed upon me. Without the grace of God, I am totally helpless. By His grace, any one of us can move mountains.

"I can't honestly explain suffering, Michael. I just know that I receive consolation as I come to understand that the Lord suffers with me, and gives me strength and hope. God's word assures us that He never abandons us. 'Are not five sparrows sold for two cents? And yet not one of them is forgotten by God. The hairs on your head are counted. Do not fear, you are more valuable than many sparrows' (Luke 12:7).

"I'm comforted in my sorrow, understanding the infinite compassion of the Lord. I may not feel His presence, but my faith assures me that He is, in fact, in the midst of my turmoil. He cries with me as He wept at the news of the death of his friend, Lazarus. 'Compassion' means 'to suffer with.' Michael, it says somewhere in the Bible, and forgive my senior moment for not remembering exactly where, but it says, 'suffering produces perseverance; perseverance, character; and character, hope' (Romans 5:4). I find great hope in the fact that no one has more compassion on me than the Lord Himself. That reality is so vital to me. It keeps me sane. Now, Michael, I hope you're not foolish enough to try and be cute and question my sanity!"

"I suspect I wouldn't survive the remainder of this journey if I even tried," Michael responded with haste. "And I really don't want to miss our visit to the Homer Spit. It's so exquisitely beautiful and my favorite part of Alaska. Although it's tempting, it's just not worth the risk!"

"Thanks be to God," sighed Irene with a broad grin on her face as she turned and quickly glanced at Michael.

"Now let me get to what I've come to understand to be at the heart of the questions you raise, particularly when you mention that so many inquire, 'How could a loving God allow such suffering?' Do you know what the greatest sin is, Michael? It's pride. 'Pride comes before the fall' (Proverbs16:8). Mankind, in his insatiable quest for answers, accepts no mysteries! We have a prideful compulsion to insist upon knowing and understanding everything. Well, it may work with science, but it doesn't always work with the will of God!

"Wasn't that the way it was in the Garden of Eden that caused Adam and Eve to fall from grace? Adam and Eve had everything they could possibly want, except for one thing: they were forbidden to eat from a single tree. And how did the clever serpent tempt Eve? Not by suggesting how delicious the fruit must be from that particular tree, as one might logically expect. No, he was much more cunning and evil in his approach. Instead, he tempted her by saying to the woman, 'You surely will not die! For God knows that the day you eat from the tree, your eyes will be opened, and you will be like God' (Genesis 3: 1-6).

"At times, we mere mortals are no better than Adam and Eve. We want to 'be like God' and have the answers to everything. No mysteries are allowed, or God forbid, our faith in Him is trashed! But God has not given it to us to eat from that tree. To develop an appetite for the fruit of that tree, gives birth to pride, whereas God loves the humble. 'Humility comes before honor' (Proverbs 18:12). The Gospel of Luke confirms that proverb, 'For everyone who exalts himself will be humbled, and he who humbles himself will be exalted' (Luke 14:11)."

"But, Mother," Michael interrupted, "haven't you ever experienced some occasions when you've felt like screaming out and asking, 'Why God?!' And if so, what do you ultimately do at those moments?" Michael sincerely inquired.

"Michael, I'd be less than honest if I didn't confess that indeed, I've experienced moments when I've cried out to God precisely as you've described. Eventually, I remember my favorite verse from Psalms, 'Be still and know that I am God' (Psalm 46:10). There are times when we just don't, can't, and won't fully understand the will of God at the moment. This is very difficult for many people to accept, because they want immediate answers to their questions and immediate resolutions to their problems, or they deny the very existence of God. In essence, they want to be like God and know and understand all of life's mysteries. However, the Bible admonishes, 'For who can know the mind of God, or who can be His counselor?' (Romans 11:34). And even more to the point, the Bible further expresses, 'For as heaven is higher than the earth, so my ways are higher than your ways and my thoughts are higher than your thoughts' (Isaiah 55:9). I seek His grace to 'be still' and I allow Him to be God, assured that my 'Father knows what I need before I even ask' (Matthew 6:8).

"Do you know what, Michael?" Irene asked rhetorically. "I think too many Christians confuse God with Santa Claus instead of their Savior! You laugh, but I'm serious," Irene chided. "I think some people believe you just make a list of everything you want, check the list twice, and then send it up to heaven stamped with a prayer! Then they expect God to deliver everything they've requested and become angry, throwing a childish tantrum, if they don't receive it all. That's just selfish ambition and not the mark of a mature walk with the Lord.

"As part of the Sermon on the Mount, our Lord says, 'How much more shall your father who is in heaven give what is good to those who ask him' (Matthew 7:11). Some people conveniently forget the emphasis on the words, 'what is good' and seek only what they want for their personal comfort. They give no regard as to whether it will further their personal holiness and salvation. The Father can only give what is good for our salvation. Sometimes, that is difficult to discern and even more painful to accept. I'm well acquainted with the pain, trust me, Michael. I experience the pain daily, but I count it a blessing.

"Many people profess to have a personal relationship with the Lord. Yet, I sometimes wonder how many of those people seek to relate personally to the Lord?"

"I'm confused," admitted Michael. "What is the distinction between those two statements?"

"Michael, I've confessed to you previously that I am no theologian by any stretch of the imagination! But I'll do my best to explain myself.

"All I'm trying to say is that unfortunately, some people seek a Gospel of personal comfort. That is why, when they experience some manner of tragedy, their faith is uprooted. They too quickly forget, that even the beloved apostle Paul, who worked many miracles recorded in the 'Acts of the Apostles', was not spared various trials and tribulations. 'We are afflicted in every way, but not crushed; perplexed, but not despairing; persecuted, but not forsaken; struck down, but not destroyed; always carrying about in the body the dying of Jesus, that the life of Jesus also may be manifested in our body' (I Corinthians 4, 8-9). Are we so fortunate that we should expect any less than the beloved St. Paul?

"On the other hand, those who seek to relate to the Lord personally, are able to empathize with His anguish in the Garden, with His passion on the cross, with His willingness to forgive His executioners. They identify with the 'Beatitudes' and the 'Sermon on the Mount' as the manner in which the Lord desires them to live their lives. It is not a Gospel of personal comfort, but one of laying down our lives daily in love for each other. It is a life that is committed to identifying and subsequently transforming our vices into virtues with the assistance of His grace.

"Indeed, it all comes down to one concise question, 'Can I relate to the Lord's singular desire and zeal to accomplish only the will of His Father?' If one can unequivocally answer that question in the affirmative, I am suggesting that they legitimately have a personally relationship with the Lord.

"I'm not implying that it is an easy task to completely abandon yourself to the love of God, trusting that He, and He alone, knows what is best for your life. It's been a real struggle for your mother, I'll readily admit. The ministry that God has bestowed on me for my life is not one I would have chosen for myself. I couldn't even have imagined it!

"However, I've discovered divine joy is truly bestowed upon those seeking and accepting His will for their lives; trusting that He will never abandon them. I couldn't begin to do that without the assurance that He has promised to go before me (Deuteronomy 31:8). I need to rely on that reality each and every day of my life, without exception. I think I would literally collapse if I did not believe that He has preceded my every step and only asks that I follow in His footsteps. Most of the time, I haven't a clue as to where He is leading me. He has shocked me on more than one occasion!

"It clearly is a matter of personal choice; an act of our free will. 'No one is taking My life from Me, I lay it down of My own free will' (John 10:18). It can be a challenging option at times, trust me! But I have found it to be the only decision that brings an abiding peace along with the grace to embrace and obediently accomplish His will, no matter how challenging."

Michael, forgetting his previous promise, interrupted once again to inquire, "Does this mean that we need not pray at all because it will ultimately be God's will that shall come to pass?"

"Oh, my Lord, nothing could be further from the truth, Michael!" responded an astonished Irene. "Saint Paul advises us to 'Be anxious for nothing, but in everything by prayer and supplication, with thanksgiving, let your requests be made known to God.' Ultimately we must seek the will of God in our lives, understanding that God promises, 'All things work together for the good to those who love God, to those who are called according to His purpose' (Romans 8:28). The operative word here is 'together.' Independently, or in isolation, we may not be able to see the good in our current circumstances. But if we wait patiently upon the Lord, ultimately we'll see how, indeed, all things have worked 'together' for the good. We may not even discover that truth until we're with the Lord in heaven, but that's the Lord's promise to us and I embrace that promise.

"In the meantime, we need to possess the humility of Mary, the mother of Jesus, who, as a young, startled woman, replied to the angel, 'Let it be done to me according to Thy word' (Luke 1:38). Do you know of a more courageous prayer?! Each time I pray those brave words, I feel as though the Holy Spirit conceives Jesus anew within me.

"Just remember one thing, Michael, absolutely nothing contradicts God's love for us! Nothing could possibly contradict His love for us because 'God is love' (John 4:8). God is the personification of perfect love and He cannot contradict Himself. This is a lesson I have learned even with great pain in my heart."

Michael read a road sign indicating that they weren't far from their destination, the Homer Spit. So, he managed to squeeze in another question for his mother. "But what about all the miracles you prayed for regarding Ricky, Dad, Maureen, and John? Aren't you at least disappointed that you didn't receive those miracles?"

"I'm astonished that you can sit there and claim that we didn't receive any miracles," responded Irene, looking over in the direction of her son. "Look at the literally thousands of people who were touched and moved deeply by the lives of John and Maureen, who spent most of their lives confined to a kitchen chair. Most of those people were more profoundly impacted by the witness of John and Maureen's faith, than by any sermon or homily they heard in their entire life! Let me ask you a few simple questions, Michael. Do you expect the church to be filled to capacity at your funeral, with all three local media stations in the church? Do you expect twenty priests to concelebrate your funeral? Do you think that if you were confined in a nursing home, that Bishops would come because of the strong presence of the Holy Spirit they had experienced in your room? Would young people be converted at your bedside and addicts instantaneously freed from their addictions?

"Enough said about that. No need to answer those questions. Those were the miracles! That was the work of God causing all things to work together to accomplish His will. I wouldn't change a thing. I praise God for those miracles!"

"You should write a book someday, Mother. You have much to share!"

"Never!" Irene replied without hesitation.

"Well, perhaps I should write one for you," responded Michael.

"Don't you dare, Michael Joseph. If you ever do such a thing, do it after I've passed. I don't want the attention!" Michael laughed, and promised his mother he would honor her request.

Michael glanced quickly at his mother and presented her with one final question with tears welling up in his eyes. "But what about all the pain you endured? I personally witnessed that pain, particularly the pain of burying three of your children and witnessing the anguishing deaths they suffered? I have images of that intense pain, written boldly across your face, indelibly marked in my heart and seared in my mind. Yet, all those who know you speak only about the sheer joy you permeate. They all testify, 'Why you wouldn't think she had a problem in the world. I don't know how she has carried on all these years?'"

Irene slapped her hand firmly on the dashboard of the car and adamantly proclaimed, "Love is stronger than pain! Don't you ever forget that, Michael."

Michael's deep thoughts about that trip to Alaska were suddenly interrupted by the sounds of Sharon, Stephen, and Patrick arriving through the front door. Michael leaped from the chair and rushed from the family room to greet his brothers and sisters with emotional sobs and strong embraces.

Michael tried to speak between his heart-wrenching sobs. "I came down a little early due to the weather, to pick Mom up and bring her over to your house, Stephen. Because I was early, I quickly fixed myself something to eat; I waited patiently for Mother to come down the stairs. Finally, I called up to her. When I didn't hear an answer, I rushed up the stairs and discovered that she had died! I just spoke with her last evening and all was well; she was very much looking forward to today."

The family quickly ascended the stairs, with Michael trailing the others. They knelt down beside the lifeless body of their mother. The weeping was incessant. The sobbing was so heart wrenching that it seemed the entire Emerald Isle had joined in mourning the loss of Irene Fitzsimons Corcoran O'Brien. The O'Brien clan, all hugging each other tightly, soaking each other's shoulders with salty tears, was indeed a deeply moving scene. It seemed so surreal to all of them. Each of the O'Brien children intrinsically knew that it was not just the plans for the day that had changed, they realized that their lives, individually and collectively, had changed forever.

After John's passing, the remaining members of the family had wished their mother would be blessed with many years of good health for their enjoyment. However, this was not in God's divine plan for her. The work that the Lord had bestowed upon Irene was finished. It was not the life the little girl from Ovid had dreamed of, nor was it the life looked forward to by a young bride in Ithaca. It was a life too impossible for anyone to have conceived. Irene lived that life with a profound obedience to the Lord. Her life served as a beacon for thousands of lost and wounded souls, guiding them to find the only true joy in life, a personal relationship with the Lord lived in the context of the Church.

Irene's funeral was meticulously planned by the family. It included hymns and Scripture readings that the family recognized as Irene's favorites. As the family sat together, finalizing all the plans, they recalled their favorite memories of their mother. Someone commented, "I don't know how she endured all she did, and yet was able to gift each of us with such a happy life as children and as adults."

Was Irene, perfect? Not by any means. She would be the first one to make that admission. However, the Bible assures us, "Above all, love each other deeply, because love covers a multitude of sins" (I Peter 4:8). The number of souls that were deeply touched by her loving, joyous spirit is a multitude that cannot be counted.

As Michael was leaving the house for the last time, he sat motionless in his car parked in the family driveway. He just starred at the house he once called home as if he was in a trance. *I remember the joy and enthusiasm the day we moved into this house. We all experienced such elation. We were a family of ten, Lord, when we moved into this house. Now we're a family of five. You took half of my family from me in the years we lived here. Four actually died agonizing deaths in this very house, making it look like a tomb to me. Were we just innocent lambs being led to slaughter, Lord?* Then he heard the words Irene proclaimed in Alaska, "Absolutely nothing contradicts God's love for us!" The words resonated so clearly, it was as if his mother was a passenger in his car once again.

Still, Michael was in deep sorrow at the loss of his mother. He seemed inconsolable as he lingered in the driveway for a few moments longer. Michael wondered how he would ever contend with the pain that was tearing at his heart. Then, once again, he heard his mother's voice, speaking with the adamancy that was uniquely her own, "Love is stronger than pain!"

Irene's had three, long stemmed, red roses gently placed atop her casket. One rose representing each of the three children she had buried. As the funeral was concluding, Irene's sons carried her casket on their shoulders as a symbol of respect for the incredible person they felt privileged to call "Mother." The hymn, "Holy God, We Praise Thy Name" was shaking the rafters of an overcrowded church.

The funeral procession picked up Route 90 until it eventually accessed Route 96A. Then, at the only blinking signal light, a very long procession of mourners made a right hand turn on the quaint Main Street in the village of Ovid. Irene had walked this street and shopped in these stores many times as a little girl, innocently dreaming of her future. This was her final farewell.

Then, when the procession reached Gilbert Road, it made a right hand turn and eventually pulled into the third driveway of Holy Cross Cemetery, almost to the end of the drive. There, on the left side, a fresh grave awaited the burial of Irene.

Irene Marie Corcoran O'Brien was laid to rest about a mile from the Gilbert House, the place of her birth. Miles could never measure the courageous walk of her life, from the day she was born, until the day she passed to glory. A simple marker, with the inscription of her name, marks the burial place of this humble woman. The irony rests in the fact that those privileged enough to know Irene Corcoran O'Brien, would readily concede that a Basilica would more appropriately recognize the heroism exemplified in her submission to the will of God for her life. A submission that was embraced with a divine joy that could only come from her complete surrender to the Holy Spirit, dwelling so fully within her.

If you are ever in the Finger Lakes region, if you are ever in Ovid, New York, Michael invites you to find Gilbert Road and Holy Cross Cemetery. You will see these markers for yourself and know the incredible story of faith that each of these markers represents. You will understand Michael's contention that the most remarkable change in Ovid, over the decades, is the brave life of one of the town's most humble daughters, named Irene.

Drink from the well of Irene's waters, that your faith may be strengthened and that you may share her conviction that, "Absolutely nothing contradicts God's love for us." Whatever pain you are enduring, the water from Irene's well shall quench your thirst, as you come to fervently believe that, "Love is stronger than pain."

Michael only asks of you a single favor. After you have prayed, please leave a single red rose upon Maureen's marker. In so doing, you will make Irene proud and you will feel richly blessed. What is more, Michael will know that you were there and that you joined him on this journey.

Lies a seed that with the Son's love, in the spring, becomes a rose.

Be still and know that I am God

Epilogue

WELL DONE GOOD AND FAITHFUL SERVANT

As Irene sat in math class, grateful that she remembered to dash back into the Gilbert House to retrieve her math book, she was distracted by the brilliant sunshine that had suddenly replaced the raging storm she had encountered earlier. She welcomed the bright rays of the sun as much as she embraced with glee the gold star she received on her corrected homework. She knew her mother would be proud of the recognition for the hard work and perseverance she expended on her challenging assignment.

Irene was summoned to the principal's office. With her homework proudly clutched in her right hand, she walked the long, dimly lit corridor toward the front of the building. *It's probably just a message from Mom about the celebration at the farmhouse. I remember her last words to me, 'When you hear your mother's voice, come home immediately'.* Upon entering the school office, radiant with the sunshine permeating the large windows, she noticed the principal speaking with a slightly bearded gentleman. Being well mannered, she did not interrupt the conversation, but waited patiently in silence for the principal to call on her.

Finally, the principal motioned Irene to approach her desk, the gentleman remained seated in front of the desk. "Irene, this is Mr. Simon Peters. He's a fisherman down at Seneca Lake. He's a friend of your father and mother."

Irene politely extended her hand to greet Mr. Peters saying simply, "It's a pleasure to meet you, sir."

Mr. Peters stood up to greet Irene. "I've heard wonderful things about you from your mother and father. It's my pleasure to finally meet you."

The principal then informed Irene that her mother had telephoned the school office, and requested special permission for her to be dismissed early to report to the farmhouse. The principal shared that Mr. Simon Peters had already taken her mother and father to the farmhouse, and had generously offered to transport her.

"Your mother was emphatic that you first stop at the Gilbert House and change into your pretty, white dress. She assured me you would know precisely which dress she was referring to. Mr. Peters will wait while you change and then take you to the stone farmhouse."

On the ride to the Gilbert House, Mr. Peters and Irene chatted as if they had known each other for a lifetime. Irene spoke about her love for Seneca Lake but confessed she was not much of a fisherman. Mr. Peters just chuckled as Irene talked incessantly to his attentive ears. She shared how, just earlier that morning, she had to walk in the most brutal storm of her lifetime just to get to school. "I must confess, there were times I didn't think I could make it, but every time such thoughts crossed my mind, I concentrated on the promise of the glory of summer yet to come!"

Mr. Peters spoke up, "Well, it sounds to me like you have fought the good fight and have finished the course, keeping the faith!" (2 Timothy 4:7).

Finally, they arrived at the Gilbert House and Irene darted inside to quickly change into her white dress. It was a long, white dress with lace around the collar. Mr. Peters remained in the car to keep it warm for her.

In a matter of minutes, she changed from her school clothing into her gorgeous, white dress. Irene stopped momentarily to brush her beautiful, dark black hair. Then, she laughed to herself as she thought, "It's only going to get messed up anyway." She checked that the door was locked behind her and then quickly returned to the car awaiting her in the driveway.

"I understand there's going to be a big celebration at the farmhouse," commented Mr. Peters.

"Oh, yes, it will be. We always have our largest celebrations at the stone farmhouse. It's very large, with a fully equipped kitchen; it has a huge dining room with the longest table I've ever seen in my life. Not to mention the spacious living room with a stone fireplace and hearth. I hope someday I can have one identical to it!"

Mr. Peters looked at Irene, once again chuckling, and said, "Well, I hope someday soon your wishes will come true, Irene! Perhaps you shall inherit one!"

As Mr. Peters pulled into the driveway of the stone farmhouse, Irene opened the door and politely thanked Mr. Peters for the ride. As she began on the walkway leading to the front porch of the farmhouse, Irene heard loud, celebratory music emanating from its stone walls. She also heard the voices of a beautiful choir. *Oh my gosh! This is a much bigger celebration than I anticipated.*

As soon as Irene reached the front door of the farmhouse, the door suddenly opened wide. The music and the choir sounded so beautiful, it permeated every atom of Irene's being. She could not help but notice a tall, strong man standing at the entrance with the most radiant face. The gentleman was dressed in white attire. Like Mr. Peters, this man was also slightly bearded. What Irene was most attracted to, were the gentleman's eyes; they were very beautiful and extremely piercing. To some extent, she felt those eyes looked familiar.

She immediately introduced herself by simply saying, "Good afternoon, sir. I'm Irene."

The gentleman responded with a smile, "I know who you are, Irene. I know you very well. Did I not tell you that, 'In My Father's house there are many rooms? If it were not so, would I have told you that I go to prepare a place for you? And if I go to prepare a place for you, I will come back and take you with Me that you also may be where I am' (John 14:2). 'Come, you who are blessed by My Father, inherit the kingdom prepared for you from the foundation of the world'"(Matthew 25:34).

As the gentleman reached out his arms to embrace Irene, she noticed a wound piercing each of his hands. She then cast her gaze upon the gentleman's feet, which were bare, and she took notice of identical wounds. Irene immediately fell to her knees, kissing the feet and the wounds of her Savior.

Jesus reached down and lovingly pulled Irene to her feet. Then, Jesus embraced Irene.

Taking her by the hand, He led her into the house. She took immediate notice that everyone was dressed in white, and she saw the choir assembled in the living room, their voices perfectly harmonious. Irene could smell the aroma of a delicious meal being prepared in the kitchen. As she glanced into the dining room, she saw that it had been arranged differently than usual. In particular, she noticed there was a head table with eight place settings and eight chairs. There seemed to be a short receiving line, standing attentively, adjacent to the head table. Other circular tables were set around the large dining room, filling it to capacity with various guests. Irene was overwhelmed as she noticed that each table had a gorgeous centerpiece filled with bundles of the most beautiful, bright orange, tiger lilies that she had ever seen!.

Jesus took Irene by the hand saying, "Come and dine with me at the head table, for you have expended your life making yourself the least of all and the servant of all." As

Irene and her Blessed Savior approached the table, they came across the receiving line.

The first person in the line was a young, strong, handsome gentleman. He was holding a glass of wine. The man raised the glass in a toast to Irene, saying, "Here's to the best mother a young man could hope for! Thank you, Mom, for everything you ever did for me. Thank you for your patience with me as I was growing up. Thank you, especially, for your daily visits and prayers during the months I was in a coma. I may have been in a coma, but your faith filled the room with such a strong presence of the Holy Spirit that I was deeply consoled. I know your heart must have ached terribly, but nonetheless you came every day to visit and pray for me. If I had one of my wrestling trophies with me, I would present it to you. You have the heart of a champion! What courage you possess, Mother! I love you!"

Irene was astonished! "Ricky!" she exclaimed. Irene took the wine glass from Ricky's right hand and set it down on a table stand, then she embraced Ricky firmly, laying her head upon his shoulder. "Oh, my goodness! How wonderful it is to see you again! Not a single day passed that I didn't think of you, my son, not a single day!" Irene held tightly onto Ricky as though she never wanted to let him go.

Next in line was yet another handsome gentleman. He had the most beautiful eyes that caused Irene to experience a sense that she had seen this man before. The gentleman spoke up and in a soft tone said, "I'm sorry I had to leave you there alone so early, Irene. I know I left you with a heavy burden to carry all by yourself, but I want you to know my gratitude for all you did for me. Thank you for every day of every year that we shared together. I enjoyed our trip to Europe immensely! Thank you for taking meticulous care of me when I was terminally ill. Thank you for taking me home from the hospital so that I could die at home, surrounded by the love of my family. You never left my side. You were so brave, why, you could have been a combat pilot in the United States Air Force! I'm certain you would have been awarded the Congressional Medal of Honor!"

"Oh, Dick!" Irene exclaimed. "I've missed you immensely! It was difficult without you, of that you can be certain. The children really assisted me; Cassie impeccably managed all of my financial affairs. And our good Lord sent plenty of wonderful "Simons" to help me carry the burden." Irene and Dick embraced.

The next two in line stepped forward together. Irene did not recognize them. There was a beautiful young woman with long, wavy hair. Standing to her left was yet another young, handsome man. The young woman was wearing a beautiful bonnet and was holding a single, red rose. As the woman handed the rose to Irene, she spoke, saying enthusiastically, "Mom! It's me, Maureen! And this is John! Look, we have no more sores! Can you believe that, Mom?

You and I are going to dance after dinner and I won't be needing my electric wheelchair!"

John stepped closer to his mother and extended his two arms and said, "Look, Mom. I even have fingers now! All ten of them! I can't wait until I can toss a football around with Jim Kelly! Ricky has been practicing with me."

Then Maureen spoke up on behalf of the two of them saying, "How could we ever adequately thank you for everything you've done for us? That would be an impossible task! There are no words. You laid down your life for us. Every day doing our dressings, preparing our special meals, being with us during our hospital visits; you lived for us. We do thank you, Mom, especially for having the courage to take us home from the hospital and blessing us with a family, despite what the doctors recommended.

"Our family gave us so much joy and love, each and every member in their own unique fashion. In the context of our family, we learned the mysteries of our faith and personally accepted our Lord and Savior. Thank you again for your bravery, your service, and your love! The words you promised to us finally came true, 'He will wipe away every tear from their eyes, and death shall be no more, neither shall there be mourning, nor crying, nor pain anymore, for former things have passed away' (Revelations 21:4)."

Irene became transformed. She was radiant! She fell to her knees and thanked her Savior. "I could never have accomplished this without Your grace and power, my Lord!"

Then Irene stood, stretched her two arms around both John and Maureen, and embraced them lovingly and tightly. It was a heavenly experience.

"Oh my darlings! You have no idea how much I've missed you! My life seemed so empty at times in your absence, I almost didn't know what to do with myself. The kitchen seemed so vacant with your empty chairs. I just couldn't get accustomed to not seeing you sitting in them. My aching heart felt as void as those two empty chairs. But your brothers and sisters took good care of me and the Lord sustained me with His daily bread. It was my joy, my honor, my privilege to care for you. It was always you who were a blessing to me! I should be thanking you. I do thank you, my darlings, from the bottom of my heart!"

The last two in the receiving line also stepped forward together. There was yet another beautiful woman standing next to a handsome man. The woman spoke up and said with warm enthusiasm, "Oh, Irene! Isn't this a grand party?"

Irene immediately recognized the raspy voice to be that of her mother. "Your father and I want to thank you for being the sweetheart you have always been to us. Even as a child, you consistently treated us with honor and respect. You were always so cheerfully obedient and assisted us in every manner conceivable. Most especially, we want to thank you for taking us into your home. When I was terminally ill, you insisted upon providing for my needs, even though you had the responsibility of caring for John and Maureen, as well as the rest of the family. My heart ached for you, my darling. How can we ever thank you sufficiently? I thought I was a strong, Irish farm girl, but you have the heart of a lioness! This is such a grand reunion! It's precisely what the Lord promised us when he said, 'No eye has seen, nor ear has heard, nor heart of man imagined what God has prepared for those who love Him!" (I Corinthians 2: 7-9).

Irene's father then spoke. "I have no need for that golden vest watch that you surprised me with on your wedding day. We are living in eternity now! There is no time! That was a concept our mere, mortal minds could not comprehend. But Irene, the inscription you engraved on the back of that watch is etched permanently on my heart! I love you dearly and can't thank you enough for all the ways in which you served me!"

"Oh, Mom! Oh, Dad! I can't describe how wonderful it is to see you again!" Irene threw herself into their extended arms for a long-awaited embrace. She insisted, "It's I who should be thanking you. We had so little, but you made us feel so rich. You taught us how to pray and how to love and serve the Lord. You never refused to come to my aid when I called for you, not a single time. I love you both so dearly. And yes, Mom, this is indeed a grand celebration! And Dad, you don't have to remind me about eternity. Why, it seems like just this morning, I was walking the entire stretch of Gilbert Road to school during that infamous blizzard of January 1934. I wish people could better realize that life on earth is but a fleeting moment compared to eternity! Even in the midst of trials and tribulations, life is no longer than the blinking of an eye compared to eternity. The words of St. Paul ring true, 'For momentary, light affliction is producing for us an eternal weight of gory beyond all comparison' " (2 Corinthians 4:17).

Then Jesus took Irene by the hand and began to lead her toward the head table. Ricky, Dick, Maureen, John, Laura, and Michael followed. As the eight were seated, people from the kitchen began serving the tables a feast surpassing anything Irene had ever witnessed in her mortal life. There was much conversation; laughter and joy permeated the room. To Irene's surprise and extreme delight, a succulent slice of plump, warm, cherry pie was served for dessert. As she immediately glanced down the table at her mother, Laura was grinning broadly, and her eyes were twinkling like brightly shining stars, as she whispered, "I baked them from scratch just for you!"

As Irene gazed upon the numerous faces in the room, she began to recognize so many of them. She recognized Dick's mother and father as well as other family members.

She was perplexed when one gentleman suddenly stood and proposed a toast, "When I was alone in the hospital you came and visited me. I wouldn't be at this celebration today if it weren't for your visits, prayers, and witnessing. Thank you for the dignity you provided me, a complete stranger, with a Christian burial." Irene was astonished to see the gentleman she had met in the hospital who had no family. The Lord leaned over and whispered in her ear, "Truly, I tell you, whatever you did for one of the least of my brothers and sisters, that you did unto me" (Matthew 25:50).

When the invited guests had finished their meal, Jesus stood. Immediately the entire house fell silent. He announced, "I have promised, 'Blessed are those who weep and mourn, for they shall be comforted. Rejoice, and be glad, for your reward in heaven is great' (Matthew 5: 4, 12). I have a gift for my guest of honor. I have saved every tear drop that Irene shed as she valiantly completed My will on earth. I have transformed each of those tears into precious gems of every variety. I have carefully embedded each of those gems in a single crown of glory."

Jesus then raised a dazzling crown that sparkled in the brilliant light. He slowly stepped behind Irene, raised the crown, and placed it carefully upon her head. Then Jesus spoke with a most appreciative voice proclaiming, "Well done, my good and faithful servant" (Matthew 25:21)!

Irene Marie Corcoran O'Brien.

A Word About My Siblings

Desmond Tutu once said, "You don't choose your family. They are God's gifts to you, as you are to them." I could not think of more genuine words when I speak about my siblings. I recognize each of them as God's gift to me, and may the Lord have mercy on me for the times I may have hurt their feelings. The Lord knows they each have deserved nothing but my love for the manner in which they have faithfully demonstrated their love for me.

I wrote this book because I felt a deep conviction that Irene's story needed to be told. I believe with my whole heart that Irene's story will inspire and console many people as they confront the tribulations of life. I am convinced that those who read Irene's story will uncover the truth, "Love is stronger than pain" and become better equipped to apply that truth to their lives by depending on the Lord for His grace and daily sustenance.

Having said that, I concede this story is told from the unique lens that constitutes the reality of my experiences and memories of the O'Brien family. Dick and Irene raised eight children. Each of us is so unique that one might marvel at the fact that we came from the same family! Isn't this usually the case? Therefore, it is entirely plausible that other members of the family could relate the same story a little differently, one that represents the unique lens of their experience as a member of the O'Brien family. Nothing would thrill me more than to read their personal account of the same story. I am confident that we would all be richly blessed.

The four Gospels reflect the singular, salvific truths of the life and mission of Jesus, each told in a slightly different manner, impacted, in part, by the unique relationship the Apostle enjoyed with Jesus. However, the essential truths confirm each other in the four Gospels. It is much the same with a family. For example, Patrick - the "caboose" of the family - was only a mere ten years old when he lost his older brother and only twelve years old when he lost his father. His experiences would be different, and probably more painful, than my experience of the same events as an adult.

I can and must state emphatically that no single one of us served Irene, Dick, Ricky, John or Maureen more than any other sibling. Without taking the risk of being specific and omitting something critical, I can unequivocally assert that everyone served equally, just differently. Everyone utilized their own unique gifts and talents in the service of the entire family, this includes the grandchildren. As Herbert Prochnow said, "There is no cure for laziness but a large family helps!" I could not possibly be prouder of my family.

One final note: Unfortunately, we live in a day and age where identity theft runs more rampant than ever. To protect my siblings, I have avoided stating their exact dates of birth and I have utilized pseudonyms in some cases.

Author's Note

This book is not intended to be considered a treatise on the disease known as epidermolysis bullosa. Rather, it is presented as the incredible story of a remarkable woman who endured much suffering, and who sought the loving presence of God in the midst of her turmoil. It is not the story of a woman who fulfilled the dreams of her childhood. Rather, it is a tale of how ultimately the joy of the Lord prevailed in her valley of tears, as she selflessly lived a life in the service of those in need. The sole intent of the story is to present the witness of a humble life, well-lived, as a means to inspire those who, inevitably, find themselves in challenging circumstances.

Research has revealed incredible new depths of information on the affliction known as dystrophic epidermolysis bullosa that was not known in the early 1950's. Today, there are many dedicated professionals who are highly skilled in the care and treatment of DEB patients. Nonetheless, it can simultaneously be a very daunting experience and one filled with joy and love. This is particularly true when afflicted patients are considered a special gift, just as every child should be considered a gift.

For additional and more current, detailed information on the disease, I would refer you to the DEBra Organization. The Mayo Clinic and Stanford University also provide detailed information on EB and DEB.

Made in the USA
Lexington, KY
15 February 2016